987 from Jay & Gill

Fisher's Comic Relief

MERRY CHRISTMAS

to Lynda

Ed Fisher

Fisher's Comic Relief

Editorial Cartoons of Arkansas in the '80's

by George Fisher

The University of Arkansas Press
Fayetteville, 1987

The University of Arkansas Press, Fayetteville, Arkansas 72701

Manufactured in the United States of America

Designer: George Fisher
Typeface: Bookman
Typesetter: Computer Graphics
Printer: Edwards Brothers

The paper used in this publication meets the minimum requirements of the American National Standard for Permanence of Paper for Printed Library Materials Ze9.48-1984.

Library of Congress Cataloging-in-Publication Data

Fisher, George, 1923 —
Fisher's comic relief.

1. Arkansas — Politics and government — 1951-
Caricatures and cartoons. 2. American wit and humor, Pictorial. I. Title. II. Title: Comic relief.
F415.F57 1987 976.7'053'0207 87-10771
ISBN 1-55728-015-0
ISBN 1-55728-016-9 (pbk.)

to
Jim Phillips
whose inspiration revived
my cartooning career

Acknowledgments

I wish to thank the following people who contributed to the production of this book:

Kay Danielson
Ernest Dumas
Keith Essex
Dorothy Harwell
Betty Lane
Marilyn Myers
Margaret Ross
Karen Wilson

Fisher's Comic Relief

CONTENTS

George Fisher's editorial cartoons

appear in the

Arkansas Gazette

Originals to the cartoons in this book
courtesy of
The Arkansas Arts Center Collection

PREFACE

Nothing dictates that history be divided neatly into ten-year periods, but each decade seems to adopt a quality of its own as if people decided when the sixties gave way to the seventies or the seventies to the eighties that it was time to confront their destinies with new, or at least different, attitudes. It has particularly seemed to fall that way with politics. The eighties brought the most dramatic change in attitudes about government in fifty years — "The Reagan Revolution," as the President's partisans call it.

Arkansas was not impervious to the changes. The same election dramatically altered the face of the state government by bringing to power, briefly, an untraditional conservative Republican. Though this Republican rule was short, the altered character of the state's politics wasn't. Four decades of modest growth ended about the time that people's ambitions seemed to awaken. It made an era of frustration.

All of it seemed to be evident in the central figure of the period, William D. Clinton. The youngest governor in America as the eighties began and an eloquent apostle of education and progress, Clinton seemed to manifest the people's hopes — and then their self-doubts as well. Alternately adroit and fumbling, bold and craven, brilliant and disappointing, Clinton had a mercurial relationship with the voters. He rallied them to support taxes, then turned them against taxes and, finally, tried to stir them to sacrifice again. But more than anything, he probably mirrored the state's own contradictory ambitions and doubts.

The passage of three-fourths of the decade, the death rattles of the Reagan Revolution and Bill Clinton's search of the distant horizon for another challenge in mid-1987 made this book and another dealing with national affairs in the Reagan era seem timely. All of the cartoons appeared in the *Arkansas Gazette*, and while they do not purport to be a historical record of Arkansas's passage through the times, I am vain enough to think that together they catch their quality and flavor.

A word or two about the idiom. Francis Bacon said that speaking in perpetual hyperbole was comely only in love, but I am sure he would have included editorial cartoons had he only known them. The artist has a greater license than the historian, the reporter, or even the commentator to range afield from the base of facts, but he exaggerates at some risk to the truth. Whether the hyperbole distills the central truth from circumstances or merely distorts is admittedly a matter on which the artist and the subjects and the viewers may disagree. The extent to which hyperbole achieves truth, I think, depends on the artist's determined fidelity to facts and to the character of the subjects and, ultimately, on his own fierce detachment. The reader may find in these pages that no politician has a corner on foible or virtue.

George Fisher

Fisher's Comic Relief

1980

The decade got off a little unsteadily. Someone named **Frank White**, who was familiar only in the Little Rock business circles where he had toiled and still little known by voters by election time, defeated Arkansas's political prodigy, **Bill Clinton**. White jumped parties to run, normally not something voters find admirable, but he inherited one good issue — an unpopular increase in car and truck license fees — and he manufactured another. Thousands of unhappy **Cubans** who had made passage to the United States on the Mariel boat lift were housed temporarily at Fort Chaffee while the government found sponsors around the country. Pent up in the compound for weeks, some of the desperate refugees got out and roamed along nearby streets. White characterized the Cuban hordes as a threat to the public order and the state's economy and their appearance on Arkansas soil as a betrayal by Clinton and his friend, Jimmy Carter. Buffeted by sharply rising **utility rates, inflation, unemployment** and **business failures**, a lot of people were in a mood to believe the worst explanations.

February 12 Southwestern Bell got a windfall when the state Supreme Court ruled that the Public Service Commission had waited too long to disapprove a rate increase, allowing the phone company to keep $7.5 million.

April 22 Governor Clinton wanted to fortify the funding of public school appropriations with extra money from an income tax windfall, but the Senate overloaded his bill with amendments and killed it.

The Balkanized Supreme Court as Proposed by the Arkansas Constitutional Convention

May 20 The Arkansas Constitutional Convention came up with a nutty plan to elect Supreme Court justices by districts so that every part of the state could have its own justice.

CONGRESS TALKS LIKE IT WANTS US BACK BUILDING DAMS, MEN! IT'S TIME TO TEST OUR FIELD PIECES!
READY...AIM... BLOW!
OLD ARMY ENGINEERS REST HOME
KEEP BUSY
TINKERS DAM
TRICKLE CREEK DAM PL
LITTLE RED RIV
WHITE RIVER DAM PLAN
BUFFALO RIVER DAM PLAN
FIRING RANGE

August 27

October 17 Frank White found his issue: Governor Clinton should have stood up to President Carter and prevented the housing of Cuban refugees at Fort Chaffee because they endangered the public safety and took jobs from Arkansans, neither of which was true.

ORVAL FAUBUS
ROSS BARNETT
GEORGE WALLACE
LESTER MADDOX
FORT CHAFFEE
IN THE TRADITION OF OTHER GREAT GOVERNORS
FRANK WHITE

October 21

October 24 Voters were sold a constitutional amendment that was supposed to save them from huge tax increases but which carried tax benefits for large landowners.

November 7 The voters denied a second term to their youngest governor ever.

... AND MAY THE MERCIFUL POWERS IN HEAVEN WATCH OVER AND PROTECT OUR WEAK SIDE TACKLES AND SPLIT ENDS.

November 30

Breaker!

December 3 White's first priority was to satisfy trucking companies and shippers and raise the weight limit on the highways to 80,000 pounds.

December 5 With electric rates rising, consumers learned that the power company had obligated them to pay for part of a giant nuclear power plant in Mississippi, called Grand Gulf.

December 21 Another teacher pay raise appropriated by the legislature didn't pan out.

1981

Anyone who doubted **Frank White's** fidelity to the principles of his new party was quickly proved wrong. His administration had little will for action — not on education, the environment, utility regulation, or even getting rid of the hapless **Cubans**, whom he had promised to banish from Arkansas soil. They stayed around for 14 months of his term before being sent to federal prisons, a shameful but fitting end to the episode. But if White had demonstrated unerring instincts as a candidate, with his hands on the reins of government every impulse proved disastrous. The most memorable, and unfortunate, was his signing, without reading, a bill requiring schools to balance the teaching of evolution with **"creation science,"** basically the biblical account of creation. It made Arkansas a national laughingstock. He never recovered his public esteem.

I'M SO SORRY MY DEAR–BUT IN THIS STORY YOU'VE GOT TO FIND A PRINCE CHARMING
PROMISED SALARY INCREASE
FRANK WHITE
ANTI-TEACHER LEGIS-LATORS
TEACHERS

February 10

the University of Arkansas Athletic Department found itself in the same financial plight as the School of Engineering?

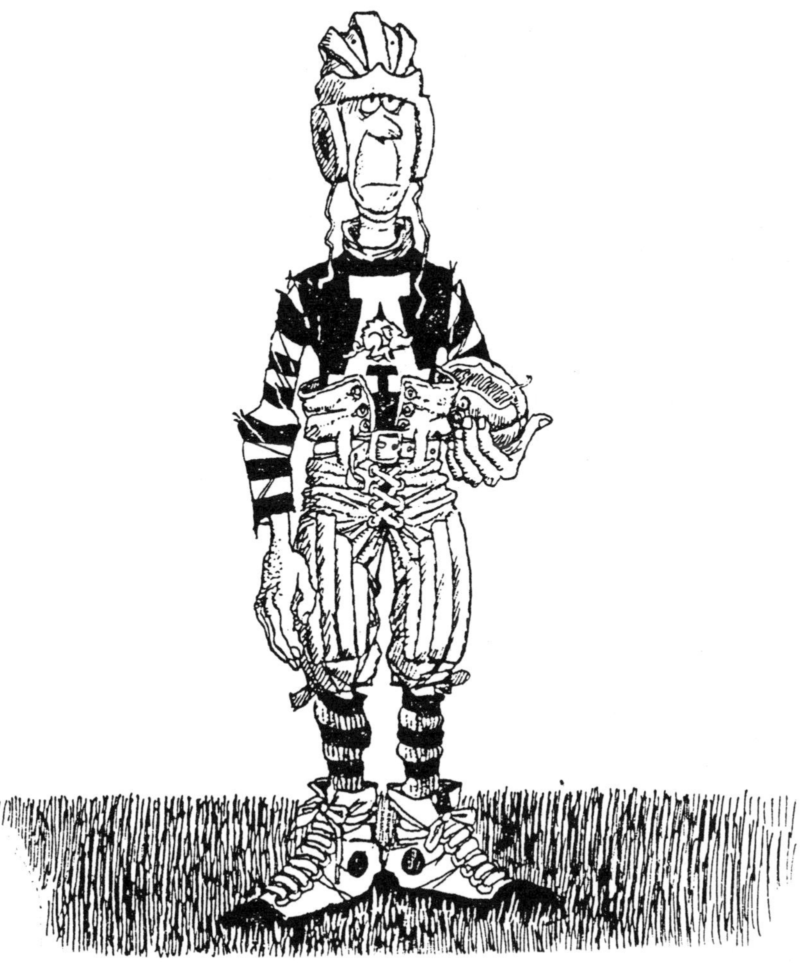

March 3

LET'S CALL IT "AN ACT TO REQUIRE BALANCED TREATMENT OF CREATION-SCIENCE AND EVOLUTION-SCIENCE"— THE GOVERNOR'LL SIGN IT
SENATE
HOUSE

March 19

March 24

SIR, I'D LIKE TO TALK TO YOU ABOUT... OH, NEVER MIND!
Arkansas POLLUTION PERMISSION COMMISSION
KEEP SULPHUR DIOXIDE EMISSION STANDARD
JARRELL SOUTHALL DIRECTOR

April 16

May 3 White wrote a letter to the director of the Governor's School, a summer program for gifted high school students at Hendrix College, complaining that the school taught "garbage" and insisting that his philosophy be substituted.

Today's Sing-along. "COOL WATER" with the Sons of the Pollut-eers
Someday you'll taste industrial waste
and think you've tasted water-r-r
COOL WATER-R-R
INDUSTRIAL POLLUTERS
POLITICS
ARKANSAS POLLUTION PERMISSION COMMISSION

July 2

GIVE ME A SHAVE, JOSÉ — BY THE WAY - WHAT ARE YOU, MEXICAN? PUERTO RICAN? SPANISH, MAYBE?
CUBAN, SEÑOR!

July 23

July 24 As the aquifer supplying water to the agricultural High Plains dwindled, Texans, including their governor, began talking seriously about acquiring Arkansas water.

WHEN ELECTED GOVERNOR I WILL STAND UP TO THE FEDERAL GOVERNMENT!
CUBAN REFUGEES FORT CHAFFEE

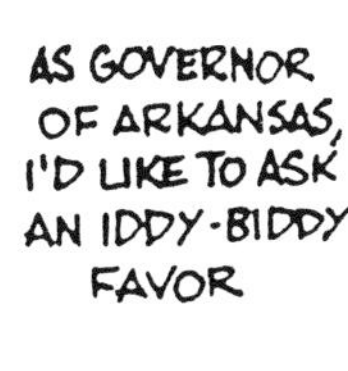
AS GOVERNOR OF ARKANSAS, I'D LIKE TO ASK AN IDDY-BIDDY FAVOR

August 26

September 2 Religious fundamentalists began to doubt that Attorney General Steve Clark, who was to defend the "creation science" law in a federal lawsuit, had his heart in it. Later, they would blame him for its being declared unconstitutional.

There once was a Governor Banana
Who dreamed up a fabulous planna
"The Cubans don't know
'Bout the ice and the snow
So let's send them up to Montana."

November 1 White was hopeful a while that the Cubans would be shipped to an abandoned air base in Montana near the Canadian border.

November 25 Arkansans began to see a lot of the new sheriff of Pulaski County, Tommy Robinson — specifically, every time they turned on the television.

December 11 When the "creation science" trial began, Arkansas had the country's attention again.

December 13 White had turned to former Governor Orval E. Faubus for advice and help in his campaign, and the courtship produced a new director of the Office of Veterans Affairs. Republicans were not enthusiastic.

FALWELL
CREATIONISTS' Garden of EDEN
TRUE BELIEVERS ONLY
Steve Clark

December 18

With an election approaching in Arkansas, the **Reagan administration** finally moved the **Cubans**, but it wasn't enough to rescue **White** from his folly, including the **"creation science"** law, which was declared unconstitutional. But White in blundering often looked no more absurd than his challengers contrived to be. **Bill Clinton** made a successful comeback by apologizing with monkish humility for nearly everything he had done his first term and posturing as a more mature and conservative politician. His major challenger at the outset was former Congressman **Jim Guy Tucker**, who also reappeared as a conservative, but in the end it was staid old **Joe Purcell** who almost sidetracked him in the primaries. Still, the show that fascinated people was not at the Capitol but at the Pulaski County Courthouse, where **Sheriff Robinson** kept at least a half-dozen feuds running at once. He led a raid on a toga party at a Little Rock hotel but misplaced the evidence before the trial, and finally set out to arrest a Little Rock lawyer for the murder of his wife, in the process taking on the prosecuting attorney, a special prosecutor, judges and a grand jury. As usual, nothing came of his efforts (three persons were convicted, none the husband) except the one outcome that counted: The sheriff became a folk hero and a major political figure.

January 22

Son of Coon Dog

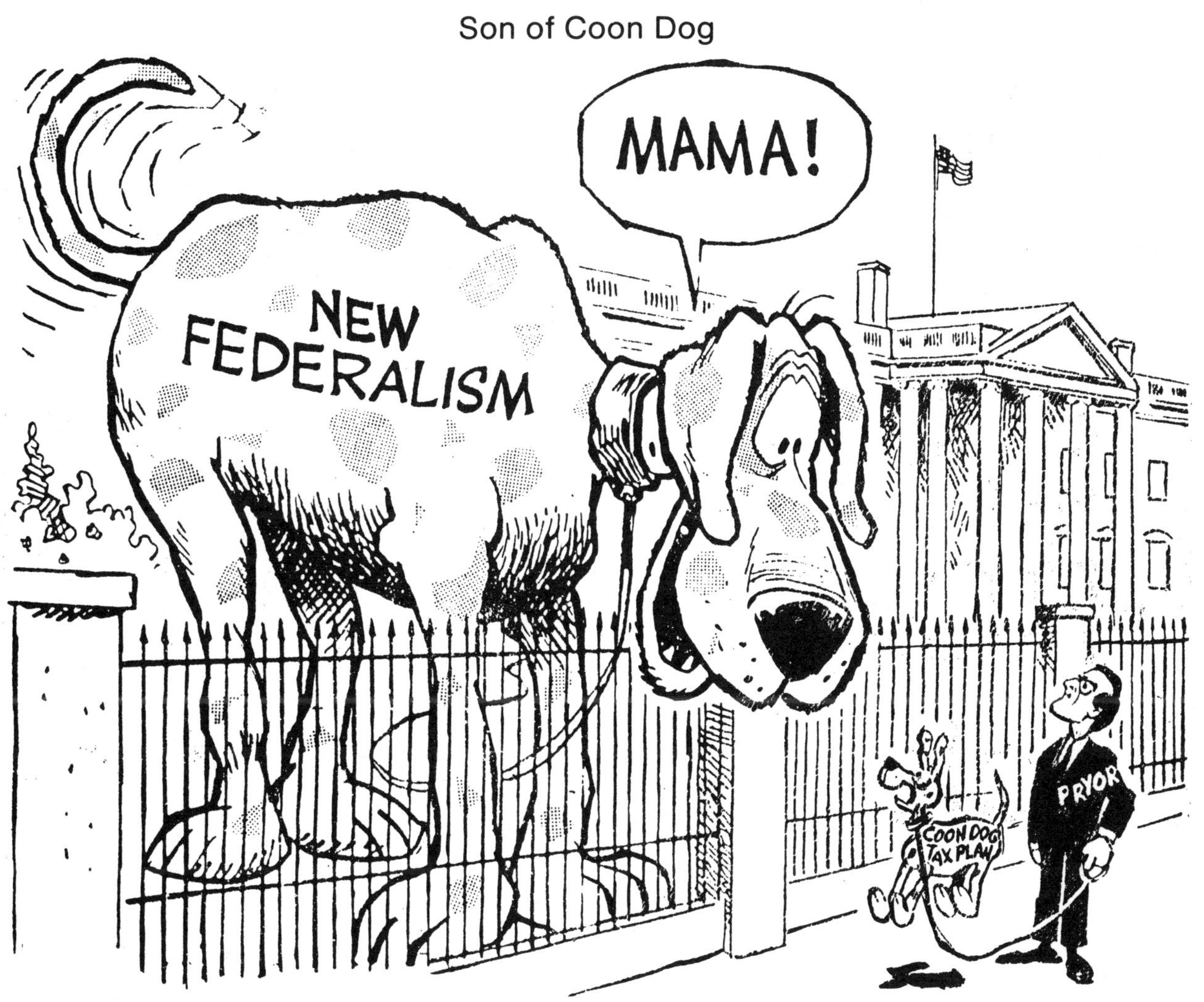

January 29 Reagan's tax cuts and his plan to refer people to state and local governments for services rather than Washington reminded many of Senator David Pryor's ill-fated "Arkansas Plan" (a.k.a. "Coon Dog Plan"), proposed in 1976 when he was governor. It would have cut state income taxes and given people the choice of raising their local taxes or else, to use his famous example, of buying a new fishing rod or a coon dog.

Good Riddance Cemetery
WHAT DID IT DIE OF?
I DON'T KNOW- I DIDN'T READ THE DEATH CERTIFICATE
ACT 590
(CREATION SCIENCE)
HOLSTED

February 7

February 18 Tucker's campaign began with a film of him in hunting garb, handling guns and talking tough about crime.

IF THESE GUYS KEEP THIS UP, IT'S GONNA MAKE FRANK WHITE LOOK ALMOST GOOD
YEAH, AND JOE PURCELL IS ALREADY LOOKING LIKE DISRAELI
LEADERSHIP BY POLLS
LEADERSHIP BY POLLS
SACK CLOTH
ASHES
RED MAN

March 18

I JUST
MIGHT
RUN
—Joe Purcell
HONEST
JOE
RED
MAN
WHO'S THE
KOOK?
SACK
CLOTH
ASHES

March 21

HOW ARE THINGS, SACK CLOTH?
SLAP
RED MAN
SACK CLOTH
ASHES
COULDN'T BE BETTER, RED MAN
SLAP
SACK CLOTH
RED MAN
ASHES
I'M A FLAMING LIBERAL
I'M A WELFARE LIBERAL

April 27

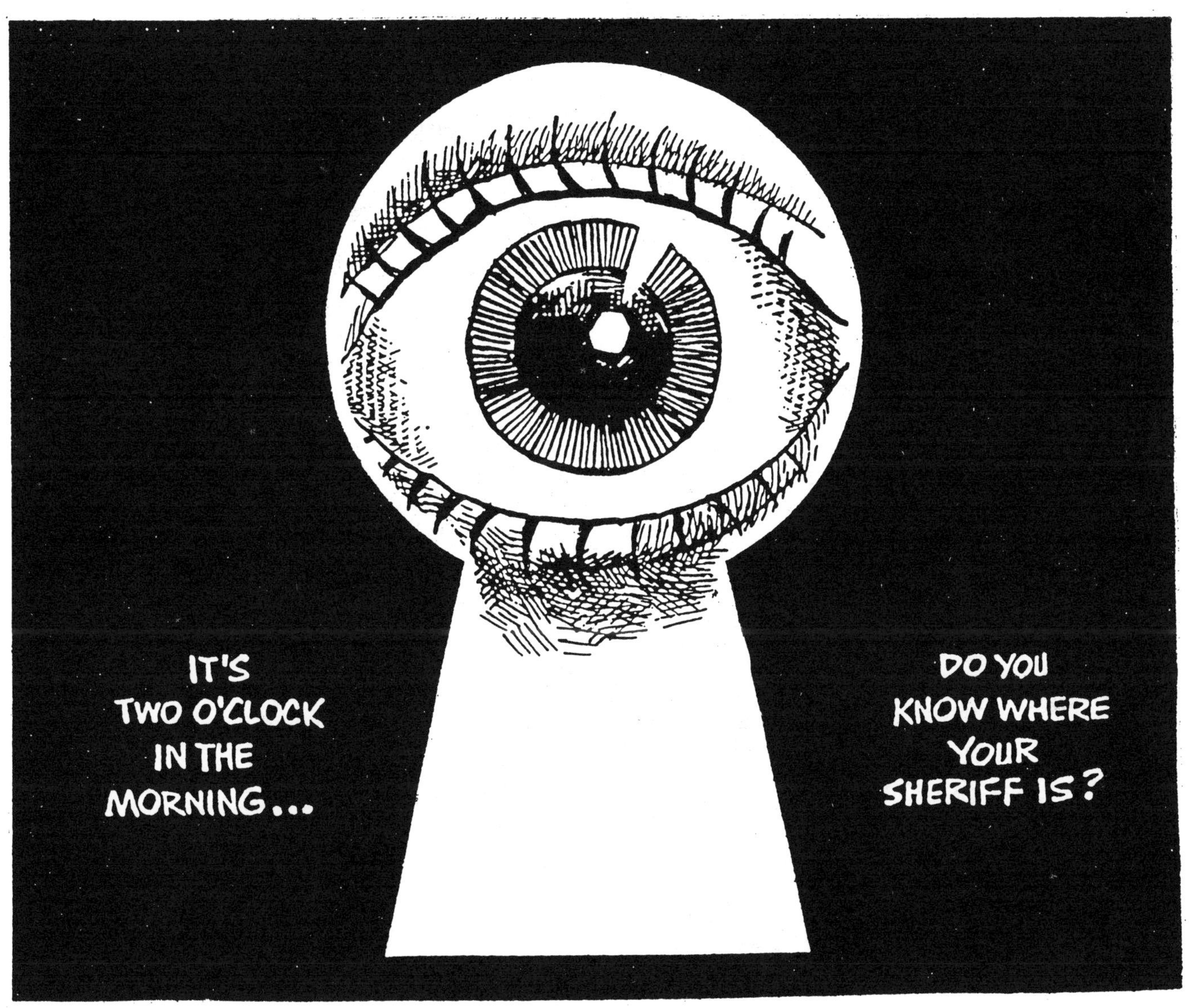

May 20 Sheriff Robinson led deputies on a raid of hotel rooms where a club called Central Arkansas Socials was having a toga party.

June 10 Clinton won the Democratic nomination.

HANG ON, MEN! ACCORDING TO THIS LIST THERE ARE 3 MORE MOTELS, A HOTEL AND A COUPLE OF GOVERNMENT BUILDINGS WHERE WE HAVEN'T PEEPED THROUGH A SINGLE KEYHOLE
TOMMY ROBINSON'S KEYHOLE KOPS

June 18

START HERE
QUARREL WITH QUORUM COURT
QUARREL WITH SHERIFF'S ASSN. – START OVER
CHAIN PRISONERS TO TOWER AND POST
CIRCLE JAIL FOR SHOOTOUT WITH POLICE
GET SUED – CALL PRESS CONFERENCE
CALL ANOTHER PRESS CONFERENCE
GO ON TV
GO ON RADIO
TIP REPORTERS
UNLEASH DRUG-SNIFFING DOG ON SCHOOLS – FIND NOTHING
GRRR!
PULL GUN ON KID FOR OBSCENE GESTURE
DROP THAT FINGER!
RASH OF JAIL ESCAPES GO BACK 3 SPACES
ARREST COUNTY JUDGE
ARREST CONTROLLER
FIRE JAIL MASTER
DEFY FEDERAL JUDGE – GO TO MEMPHIS JAIL
APOLOGIZE AND GET OUT OF JAIL
CALL PRESS CONFERENCE and SLUR BLACK FEDERAL JUDGE
OVERSPEND YOUR BUDGET – ASK FOR MORE
FIRE DEPUTIES
GET SUED – GO BACK 3 SPACES
GO TO BAHAMAS WITH MORAL MAJORITY
ACCUSE TROUTT PUBLICLY
GO TO CENTRAL AMERICA
COME BACK EMPTY-HANDED
ARREST TROUTT AT 3 A.M.
GET ACCUSED OF BEATING TROUTT
FREE TROUTT
ARREST TROUTT AGAIN
ARREST TROUTT EMPLOYEE
GET ACCUSED OF BEATING TROUTT EMPLOYEE
TAKE LIE DETECTOR TEST
PASS TEST – CALL PRESS CONFERENCE
LIE
TRUTH
RAID A TOGA PARTY
GET RE-ELECTED
GET SUED
GO ON TV
DENOUNCE PRESS
HINT SUPREME COURT JUDGE CRIMINAL
CHARGE SUPREME COURT JUSTICES WITH KNOWING TROUTT
CALL PRESS CONFERENCE
GET CALLED HITLER BY SUPREME COURT JUDGE
FRY TROUTT
KEYHOLE KOPS
A TOMMY ROBINSON GAME

June 22

July 2

July 25 Pryor signed on as a supporter of Reagan's constitutional amendment to force a balanced budget.

SIRS-
I'D LIKE TO
REPORT A
VERY SERIOUS...
OH, NEVER
MIND
PULASKI
COUNTY
CRIMINAL
JUSTICE
SYSTEM
DEPOSITION
LEAKS
WITNESS
TESTIMONY
TESTIMONY
TESTIMONY
OF
LEAKS
LEAKS
LEAKS
DEPOSITION
POLICE!

September 7

November 4 Triumph over Frank White, another graduation.

HMMM! I DON'T KNOW IF WE CAN TAKE REPUBLICANS AND I'M NOT SURE YOU'VE SUFFERED ENOUGH - HOWEVER, AS CHAIRMAN OF THE POLICY COMMITTEE, I'LL BE GLAD TO TAKE YOUR APPLICATION UP WITH MY BOARD OF DIRECTORS.
WHO'S THE FUNNY LOOKIN' GUY WITH THE BANANA?
DUMMY- DON'T YOU KNOW NOTHIN'? THAT'S GOV'NOR WHITE! HE WANTS TO JOIN
BUT IS HE A BONAFIDE VET'RAN? HAS HE EVER FACED THE WITHERING CROSS FIRE OF POLITICAL HELL? HAS HE EVER SUFFERED THE AGONIES OF...
NAH! THE ONLY RACE HE EVER WON WAS AGAINST A KID ON A TRICYCLE
ASININE!
DOOR BELL
MUTT-MARLIN
MARION-JIM
CASEY-PAUL
-DALE
GLENN-BOYCE
MILT
OLD GUARD REST HOME

November 7

November 23 Clinton sent the Legislative Council a grim budget.

December 8 Historic floods hit much of the state.

1983

The new **Bill Clinton** of the 1982 campaign turned out to be the real McCoy. In office again, he was reluctant, compromising, moderate on all things. Little was done about the state's educational needs at the regular legislative session except for a bill ordering new accreditation standards for the schools, which the governor decided to endorse as it was passing the House of Representatives. Legislative leaders talked about pushing a tax program of their own without the governor. After the **Supreme Court** invalidated the state school finance system in the summer, virtually mandating a large tax increase, and his wife, **Hillary**, caused a popular demand for school reform as chairman of a committee that was to write new school standards, Clinton finally called a special session in the fall and proposed an array of taxes and school programs. At the **Pulaski County Courthouse**, bedlam reigned and the making of a congressman continued.

January 6 Robinson baited Prosecutor Dub Bentley daily, hinting that he might just arrest the prosecutor.

January 12 As Clinton was sworn in, one of the big questions was whether he would keep the most famous member of the White administration.

OLD GUARD REST HOME
BEFORE WE DO THE RUFFLES AND FLOURISHES, FOLLOWED BY THE STIRRING STRAINS OF DIXIE, LET ME SAY, IN BEHALF OF ALL OF US, WELCOME BACK, ORV! THE BLUE KNIGHT ROOM AWAITS YOU!
CLINTON
HI! I'M GLENN WALTHER
ASININE!
CIGARS
XXX

January 27

January 28 Religious groups sought exemption in the legislature from the state regulations for child-care centers. Among other things, they wanted to use corporal punishment.

February 4 Even judicial orders didn't deter Robinson, especially if they tried to keep him away from the TV cameras.

February 6 Robinson had a vision in the night and arrested lawyer Bill McArthur for suspicion in the murder of his wife.

Now Showing* IN PULASKI COUNTY
GREATEST SHOW ON EARTH
DING-A-LING BROS. CIRCUS
CLOWNS! CLOWNS! CLOWNS!
TIGHTROPE WALKING
BELLY DANCING
SEE AND HEAR WORLD'S GREATEST
LYIN' ACT
JUGGLING
HOT POTATOES
SEE HUMAN CANNONBALLS
TRAVEL 45 MILES IN 21½ MINUTES
MALVERN

February 16

TAX THE TRUCKS
ARK. HIGHWAY DEPT.
GOVERNOR CLINTON
HAVE A NICE DAY
NO TRUCK TAXES
TRUCK LOBBY
GOVERNOR CLINTON
HAVE A NICE DAY
NO TRUCK TAXES
TRUCK LOBBY
TAX THE TRUCKS
TRUCK LOBBY
ARK. HIGHWAY DEPT.
WHAT WERE YOU SMILING FOR?
I WAS GOING TO ASK YOU THE SAME THING!
TAX THE TRUCKS

March 2

HIGHWAY FINANCES
SEVERANCE TAX REFORM
SCHOOL FUNDING
PRISON PROBLEMS
SPECIAL INTERESTS
LEGISLATURE

March 4

March 22 Adding injury to insult, taxpayers had to pay the legal fees of striking down the "creation-science" law.

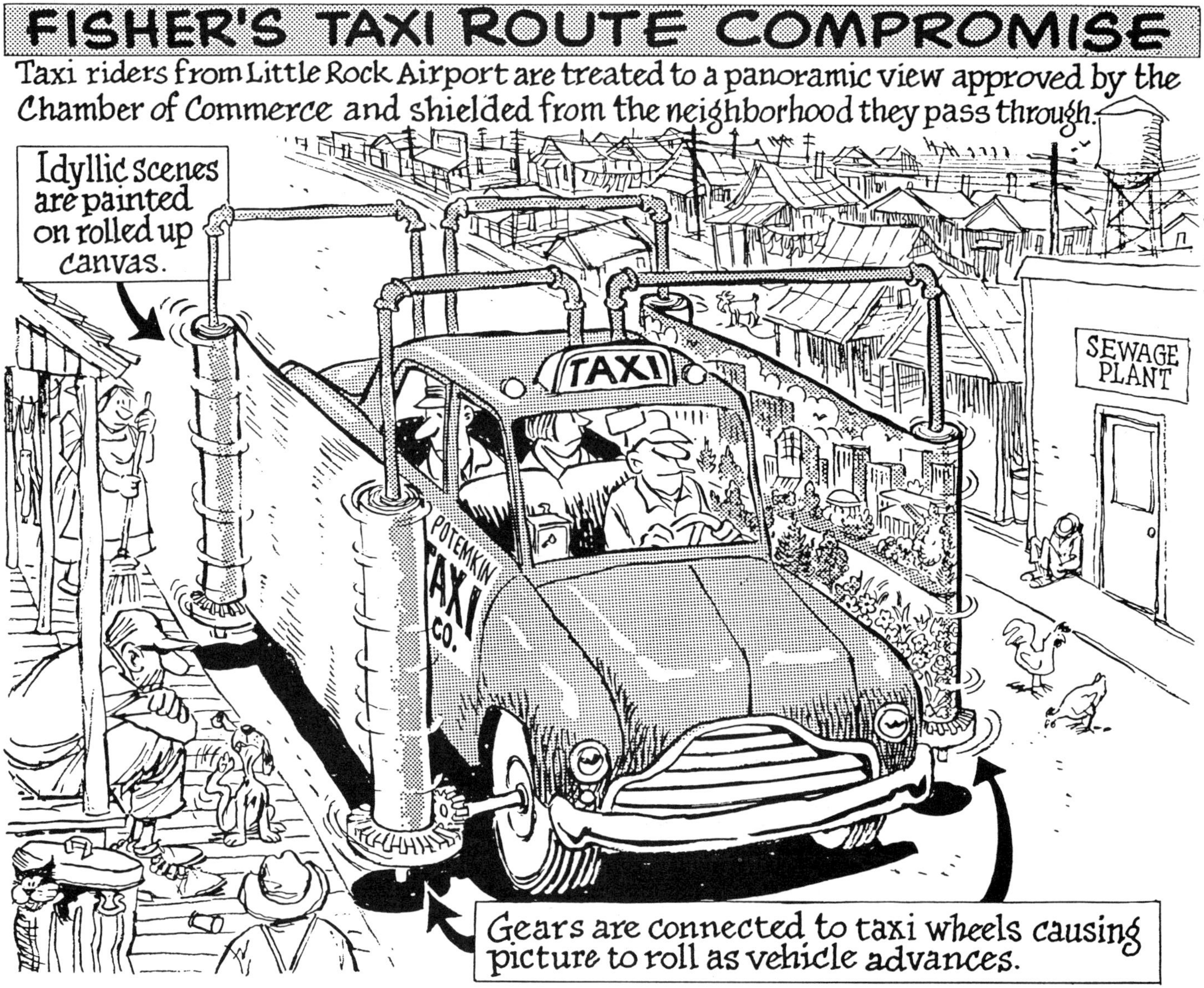

FISHER'S TAXI ROUTE COMPROMISE

Taxi riders from Little Rock Airport are treated to a panoramic view approved by the Chamber of Commerce and shielded from the neighborhood they pass through.

Idyllic scenes are painted on rolled up canvas.

TAXI

POTEMKIN TAXI CO.

SEWAGE PLANT

Gears are connected to taxi wheels causing picture to roll as vehicle advances.

March 24 The chamber of commerce wanted the city to direct taxis to take passengers from the airport along a scenic route to downtown rather than by the short route through poor neighborhoods.

March 31 The city Board considered a billboard ordinance, given impetus by the appearance of huge, fleshy billboards.

ANTI-CONSOLIDATION
20th CENTURY
THANK GOD FOR ARKANSAS
MISS.

April 1

May 24 Clinton couldn't make up his mind about a special legislative session on the schools.

June 3 The state Supreme Court invalidated the state school finance system and ordered the state to equalize educational opportunity.

GOOBERS
AS OUR LEADER, HOW DO YOU STAND ON SCHOOL CONSOLIDATION?
I HAVE A COMMITTEE LOOKING INTO IT!
IF YOU CALL A SPECIAL SESSION, WILL YOU RECOMMEND CONSOLIDATION?
I HAVEN'T RULED OUT **VOLUNTARY** CONSOLIDATION, YET.
A LOT OF FOLKS ARE SAYING WE HAVE FAR TOO MANY TINY SCHOOL DISTRICTS. SO WHY ARE WE HOLDING BACK?
IF EVERY VOTER AND LEGISLATOR WOULD GO ALONG, I'D CERTAINLY GIVE IT SERIOUS CONSIDERATION.
BUT CAN SCHOOLS OFFER EQUAL PROGRAMS WITHOUT CONSOLIDATION?
MAYBE OR MAYBE NOT— BUT I'M NOT SURE IT'S ABSOLUTELY NECESSARY
I HOPE I'M NOT ASKING YOU TOO MANY BOTHERSOME QUESTIONS.
NOT AT ALL— HOW ARE YOU GOING TO LEARN MY POSITION IF YOU DON'T ASK QUESTIONS?
GOOD OLD WISHY-WASHY!

June 14

MY POINT IS, SIR, THAT MOST GOVERNORS DON'T LOOK LIKE THAT — AND MAY I MAKE A SUGGESTION?
Captain Flame
ARKLA
ARKLA POLL
SHEFFIELD NELSON
PRESIDENT AND
CHAIRMAN of the BOARD

June 23

GOOBERS

June 28

"Life goes on after football - the state should deny extra-curricular activities to students who don't meet grade standards."
THAT'S PRETTY BOLD TALK— WHO SAID THAT?
YOUR WIFE

July 6

July 15 Secretary of State Paul Riviere let it be known he would seek the congressional seat of Ed Bethune.

August 19 Out of office, Frank White became a statesman.

TO LEAD OR NOT TO LEAD—THAT IS THE QUESTION—
WHETHER 'TIS NOBLER IN MIND TO SUFFER
THE SLINGS AND ARROWS
OF OUTRAGED SPECIAL INTERESTS
OR TO TAKE ARMS AGAINST
A SEA OF TROUBLED CONSTITUENTS...
FOR WHO WOULD BEAR THE WHIPS
AND SCORNS OF CLARENCE BELL
AND LLOYD GEORGE?
THUS THE LEGISLATURE
DOTH MAKE COWARDS
OF US ALL!

August 21

AWRIGHT, MEN! MOST ALL OF OUR MEMBERS AGREE THAT FRANK HAS GOT TOO LIBERAL FOR THE OLD GUARD REST HOME. IT'S TIME FOR A VOTE ON WHETHER OR NOT HE STAYS!
WHY, HE'S AN OUT-AND-OUT EXTREMIST! I SAY WE BOUNCE 'IM CLEAN BACK TO LITTLE ROCK!
GENTLEMEN, I BESEECH YOU NOT TO JUDGE OUR BROTHER SO HARSHLY! LET HE WHO HATH NOT STRAYED ONTO THE PATH OF WICKED MODERATION CAST THE FIRST STONE—UH, NOT YOU, JIM. I, FOR INSTANCE, ONCE ENROLLED IN A COMMUNIST COLLEGE; SUPPORTED THE GREAT SOCIETY, LYNDON JOHNSON AND MENTAL HEALTH. AND YES, I RAISED TAXES—NOT ONCE BUT SEVERAL TIMES. LET US NOT ABANDON THE MILK OF HUMAN KINDNESS IN THIS HALLOWED HOME.
OUR FOUNDER HAS SPOKEN! I MOVE WE SPUNGE THE ARTICLES OF EXPULSION!
WELL, OKAY BUT WE OUGHT TO MAKE HIM JOIN BANANAS ANONYMOUS
SNIFF! WHIMPER
BLESS THE DAY I APPOINTED HIM DIRECTOR OF VETERANS AFFAIRS
ASININE!
ACE Funeral Home
EXCUSE ME—I'M HAVING AN ATTACK OF NAUSEA!

August 24

August 26 The artist's wife, the "Snooky" of all his cartoons, died.

October 14 Much of the state's scarce resources propped up small schools, which had huge overhead.

November 11 The legislature passed Clinton's sales tax but not the rest of his tax plan for the schools.

November 13 Sap doesn't rise until spring but political juices now stir at the approach of winter.

THE HEADLINES COULD READ, "JUSTICE JIM RETURNS TO ARKANSAS'S HIGHEST COURT," OR "SENATOR JOHNSON SWORN IN, REPLACING THAT MESS OF TRASH."
I FEEL I CAN'T DISAPPOINT MY FRIENDS WHO HAVE URGED-YES-EXHORTED, ME TO SEEK THE OFFICE OF SECRETARY OF STATE!
ARKANSAS VOTERS JUST MIGHT RETURN ITS LIBERAL, SILVER-TONGUED ORATOR TO THE HALLS OF CONGRESS!
WHAT'S GOIN' ON HERE?
JIM, ORV AND ALFORD ARE OFF FOR LITTLE ROCK TO LEAK THEIR POSSIBLE CANDIDACIES FOR PUBLIC OFFICE.
HOLD IT, MEN! I HEARD ON THE RADIO THAT SHER'FF TOMMY ROBINSON SAID, DON'T COME TO LITTLE ROCK WITHOUT A GUN! THAT PLACE IS A HOTBED OF CRIME AN' VIOLENCE! WHY CAN'T YOU MAKE YOUR LEAKS IN OPPELO OR BLUE BALL?
THEN THEY NEED ME, AS A FORMER SHER'FF, TO GO ALONG FOR PROTECTION-WE DON'T WANT NO MEMBER OF THE OLD GUARD REST HOME VICTIMIZED BY CRIME CITY!
ASININE! THEY COULD MAKE THEIR LEAKS IN ARGENTA WHERE ALL IS PEACE AN' TRANQUILLITY!
WHOOPEE! ALERT THE MEDIA!
U.S. SENATE RULES
JUDICIAL ROBE

December 11

1984

In the spring, a United States district judge ordered the consolidation of the three school districts in Pulaski County to end segregation, and it shaped the state's politics like nothing had since the confrontation at Central High School 27 years earlier. If he was not already headed there, it installed **Tommy Robinson** in the United States House of Representatives. Already the tribune of people in the cocklebur country outside the city for his wild behavior as sheriff, Robinson made himself the savior of those in the suburban precincts as well by denouncing the decision and the whole federal judiciary and promising to put an end to it all when he got to Washington. Other politicians discovered the issue, but too late, for it would accommodate only one demagogue at a time. The GOP's star, Congressman **Ed Bethune**, tried desperately to exploit it in his race against Senator **David Pryor** but neither that nor anything else, including the rising issue of paying for a giant Mississippi power plant, would serve any of the Arkansas Republicans in 1984.

January 13 Former Congressman Ray Thornton, a perennial prospect for senator or governor, was appointed president of the University of Arkansas, leaving clearer horizons for the state's major officeholders.

THEM TWO ARE GONNA OVERDO IT, CHASIN' AROUND THE YARD ALL DAY LONG!
NOT AT ALL! I SUGGESTED TO BOYCE THAT HE SHOULD HELP HIS BROTHER GET IN SHAPE FOR HIS UPCOMING RACE FOR CONGRESS!
WHAT'S MUTT DOIN' MAKIN' THEM LITTLE STICKERS WITH ALFORD'S NAME ON EM?
I GUESS WE OUGHTA TELL HIM THAT THIS TIME DALE'S RUNNING AS A BONY-FIED DEMOCRAT—NOT AS A WRITE-IN OR A STICK-ON. HE'S FOR ALL THEM PROGRAMS FOR THE POOR, THE NEEDY, THE DOWN-AND-OUT!
NO LILY-LIVERED LIBERAL OR A BLEEDING HEART DO-GOODER CAN GET ELECTED TO CONGRESS
ASININE! NOW, WHO COULD BE MORE DOWN-AND-OUT THAN WE ARE?
OLD GUARD REST HOME
DR. DALE ALFORD FOR CONGRESS
TRAINER
THE EYE DOCTORS JUST MIGHT MAKE A SPECTACLE OF THEMSELVES

January 18

MARLIN, MUTT, JIM AND ORV ARE JUST BACK FROM A HIGH LEVEL SEMINAR WHERE THEY DISCUSSED THEIR ROLES IN ARKANSAS POLITICS! THEY HAD A BIG TIME KICKIN' AROUND THE ARKANSAS GAZETTE!
THEY KNOW THE GAZETTE, ALL RIGHT- I COULDN'T HAVE SELECTED A WISER PANEL MYSELF!
I TOLD THE CROWD I DIDN'T APPRECIATE THE GAZETTE CALLING MY ORGANIZATION A CORRUPT MACHINE. I JUST DON'T KNOW WHERE THEY GOT THOSE NOTIONS!
I GET MY DANDER UP WHEN THEY TALK ABOUT THE OLD GUARD. WHAT ABOUT ALL THE GOOD THINGS WE DID?
OLD GUARD REST HOME
THE NEWSPAPERS QUITE FREQUENTLY CALL UPON ME TO WRITE A FAIR-MINDED, UNBIASED COLUMN ON IMPORTANT ISSUES, BUT I JUST CAN'T PENETRATE THE THICK SKULLS OF THOSE SQUIRREL-HEADED EDITORS AT THE AR-KIN-SAW GAZETTE!
GENTLEMEN-LET US NOT BE TOO HARSH ON THE FOURTH ESTATE. I FIND THEM QUITE RECEPTIVE TO MY LIBERAL LEANINGS AND PROGRESSIVE IDEAS!
ALFORD FOR CONGRESS
ASININE!
AS I TOLD THAT FINE, LEARNED AUDIENCE, THE GAZETTE WAS ALWAYS BENT ON DRAGGING OUT THE BAD THINGS, WHILE OVERLOOKING THE STERLING, BENEVOLENT DEEDS OUR SERVICES RENDERED!
OTHER THAN THAT, MRS. LINCOLN – HOW DID YOU LIKE THE PLAY?

April 1

TWO FEWER MOUTHS TO FEED—FIRST, ALFORD LEAVES TO CAMPAIGN FOR CONGRESS, AND NOW JUSTICE JIM HEADS OUT TO RUN FOR **CHIEF JUSTICE OF THE SOO-PREEM COURT.** WHO SAID THESE BOYS ARE **OVER THE HILL?**
YEAH- AND HE FILED AS A **REPUBLICAN!** I AIN'T GOT NO USE FOR A **TURNCOAT!** I GOT A PRETTY GOOD IDEA HE'LL BE BACK!
AND WHEN HE **DOES,** WE'LL PUT HIM IN TH' **LEAN-TO** WITH THAT OTHER REPUBLICAN, FRANK WHITE!
DON'T BE TOO HARD ON HIM, GENTLEMEN—LET'S FACE IT—THE G.O.P. IS WHERE THE **MONEY'S** AT—BESIDES, HIM AND CRANK NEVER COULD BEAT A REPUBLICAN!
JIM—I'M DELIGHTED! YOU'RE RUNNING AS A **REPUBLICAN!** IF THERE'S ANYTHING I CAN DO...
DON'T DO ME ANY FAVORS, FRANK—ON SECOND THOUGHT, YOU MIGHT SET ME UP WITH **WITT** AND **JACK!**
AN INFUSION OF NEW BLOOD! IS ARKANSAS READY FOR IT?
ASININE!
OLD GUARD REST HOME

April 6

And now, ladies and gentlemen—the Second Congressional District's

1984 Overture

April 8 The field in the Second District congressional race tuned up: (from left) Secretary of State Paul Riviere, Jim Taylor, Thedford Collins, Dr. Dale Alford, Judy Petty, Stanley Russ and Tommy Robinson.

WHAT'S JIM DOIN' HERE? AIN'T HE SUPPOSED TO BE OUT CAMPAIGNIN' FOR THE SOO-PREEM COURT?
HE JUST STOPPED BY TO COOL HIS HEELS AN' HIS HEAD, 'CAUSE HE THINKS THE GAZETTE CAJOLED JUDGE WOODS INTO CONSOLIDATIN' PULASKI COUNTY SCHOOLS!
IT'S AN OUTRAGE! THAT SCANDALOUS RAG IS OUT TO DESTROY THE PUBLIC SCHOOL SYSTEM AS WE KNOW IT! THEN THOSE REPORTERS TRIED TO SHAME ME, ASKING IF I WAS A SEGREGATIONIST BACK IN THE GOOD OL' DAYS! I SAID YES, BUT BACK THEN IT WAS THE LAW OF THE LAND! JUSTICE JIM, I RETORTED, HAS ALWAYS STRUCK HIS GAVEL ON THE SIDE OF THE LAW!
JIM - YOU REPUBLICANS NEVER GET YOUR FACTS STRAIGHT - WHEN YOU WERE RABBLE-ROUSIN', SEGREGATION WAS NO LONGER THE LAW OF THE LAND!
MAYBE HE PREFERS TO ABIDE BY THE 1896 PLESSY-FERGUSON DECISION - OR EVEN DRED SCOTT!
I HAVE NO QUALMS ABOUT THE POSITION I TOOK BACK THEN. AS GOVERNOR, I WAS ABIDING BY THE WISHES OF THE PEOPLE. I DIDN'T HAVE TO EQUIVOCATE ON THE RAMIFICATIONS OF STICKY LAW!
OLD GUARD REST HOME
ASININE!
"JUST BECAUSE I SAID IT, DOESN'T MAKE IT SO."

April 18

April 29 A federal judge's order to consolidate the schools in Pulaski County brought out the state's firebrand segregationist, former state supreme court Justice Jim Johnson.

TOMMY ROBINSON DRESSED UP LIKE ABE LINCOLN! WHAT'S THAT ALL ABOUT?
IT'S BECAUSE HE SAYS HE AND ABE HAD PARALLEL ROLES IN THEIR STRUGGLES FOR HONOR AND DECENCY!
IF HE'S ABE LINCOLN, I'M WYATT EARP!
I WOULDN'T BE OFFENDED IF YOU SIMPLY ADDRESSED ME AS HONEST TOM!
TOMMY ROBINSON for CONGRESS
I DON'T WANT TO SOUND PRETENTIOUS, BUT MANY OBSERVERS HAVE COMPARED MY TENURE IN OFFICE TO THAT OF FRANKLIN DELANO ROOSEVELT'S!
HOW MANY TIMES HAVE I HEARD IT? "JIM," THEY'D SAY, "YOU HAVE ALL THE INTREPID BEARINGS OF ROBERT E. LEE AND THE SPLENDROUS STATURE OF JOHN C. CALHOUN!"
JUSTICE JIM FOR SUPREME COURT
ARE YOU SURE THEY DIDN'T SAY SENATOR BILBO?
DARE I SAY IT? THOSE WHO KNOW ME BEST HAVE CHARITABLY MENTIONED MY LIBERAL JEFFERSONIAN QUALITIES!
DALE ALFORD for CONGRESS
OLD GUARD REST HOME
JUST CALL ME LASSIE
ASININE!

May 1

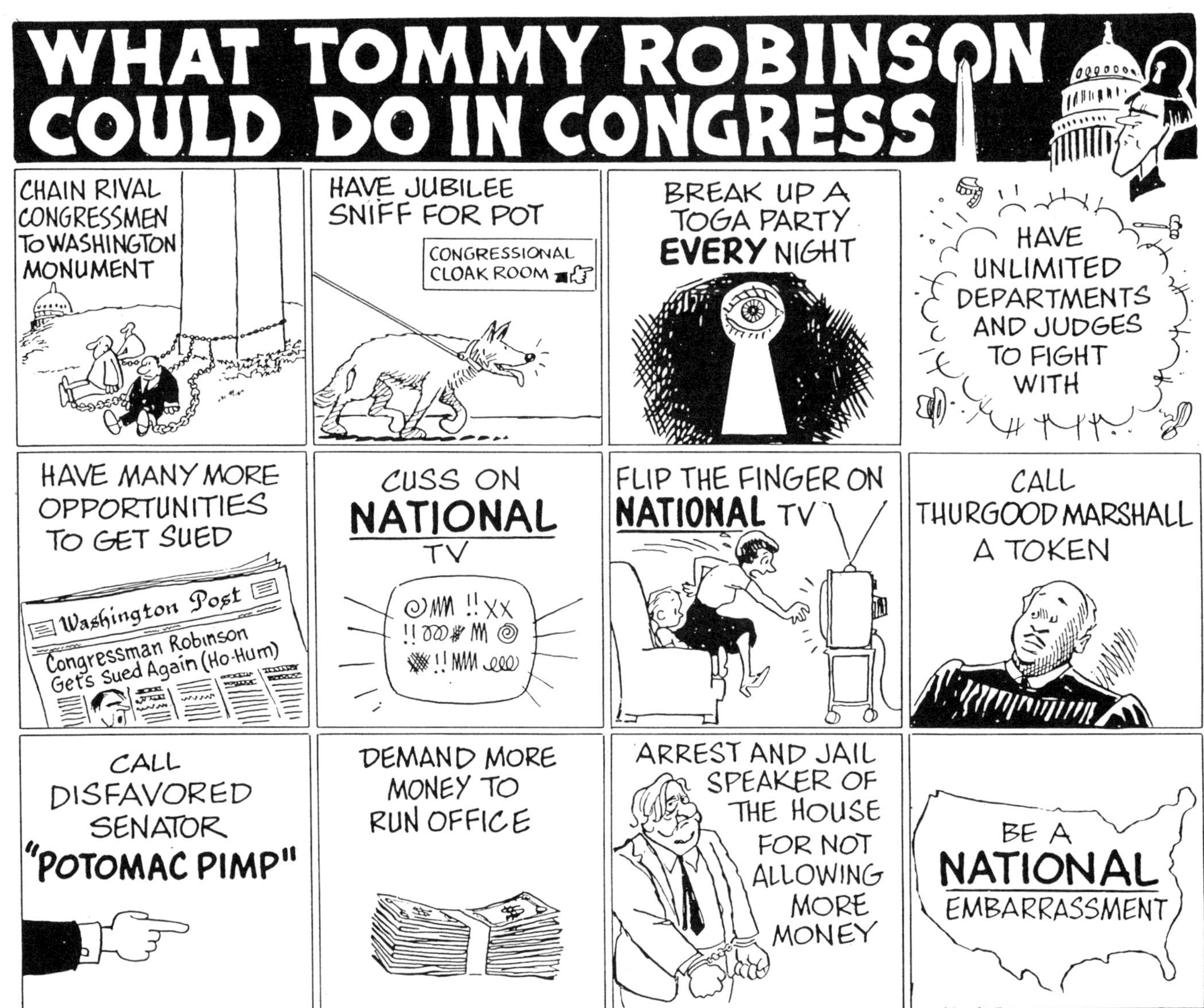
WHAT TOMMY ROBINSON COULD DO IN CONGRESS
CHAIN RIVAL CONGRESSMEN TO WASHINGTON MONUMENT
HAVE JUBILEE SNIFF FOR POT
CONGRESSIONAL CLOAK ROOM
BREAK UP A TOGA PARTY EVERY NIGHT
HAVE UNLIMITED DEPARTMENTS AND JUDGES TO FIGHT WITH
HAVE MANY MORE OPPORTUNITIES TO GET SUED
Washington Post
Congressman Robinson Gets Sued Again (Ho-Hum)
CUSS ON NATIONAL TV
FLIP THE FINGER ON NATIONAL TV
CALL THURGOOD MARSHALL A TOKEN
CALL DISFAVORED SENATOR "POTOMAC PIMP"
DEMAND MORE MONEY TO RUN OFFICE
ARREST AND JAIL SPEAKER OF THE HOUSE FOR NOT ALLOWING MORE MONEY
BE A NATIONAL EMBARRASSMENT

May 10

May 22 Robinson hired the state's largest advertising agency and became a model of self-control.

WHAT IN TARNATION HAPPENED TO ALFORD?
HE GOT CAUGHT IN TH' POLITICAL CROSS-FIRE IN DISTRICT 2.
HE NEEDS A DOCTOR BAD!
BUT HE IS A DOCTOR-WELL HE'S AN EYE DOCTOR! WE COULD SEND FOR THAT OL' VETERINARIAN DOWN TH' ROAD!
THE FIGHT'S NOT OVER UNTIL THE LAST SHOT'S FIRED – I SAY WE (COUGH, COUGH) RELOAD AND MAN THE REDOUBTS!
IF YOU HAD RUN AS A REPUBLICAN, ALFORD, YOU COULD'VE HAD 6 MORE MONTHS OF FUN!
MY SECRET FARKLEBERRY ELIXIR AND A FEW BAND AIDS WILL FIX HIM UP IN NO TIME!
CONGRESSIONAL RACE? ASININE! MINOR LEAGUE STUFF! I'M GOIN' DOWN TO TH' STORE AN' FIND OUT HOW TH' BIG RACE CAME OUT IN ARGENTA!
OLD GUARD REST HOME
AROUND HERE, IT'S NOT WHETHER THEY WIN OR LOSE, BUT HOW LONG IT TAKES THEM TO HEAL!

May 31

IF ANYONE ASKS, JUST SAY YOU'RE A WHIZ AT FUND-RAISING!
BANKERS
AP&L
ARKLA
MIDDLE SOUTH
GRAND GULF
OIL and GAS FAT CATS
TR FOR CONGRESS
$
$
$
$
$

June 5

PIT STOP

June 7 Robinson set a record for spending in an Arkansas congressional race, helped by more than 120 gifts from Middle South Utilities and its contractors and suppliers.

June 15 A Federal Energy Regulatory Commission law judge ruled that AP and L could not back out of its commitment to Middle South to help pay for a $3.5 billion nuclear power plant in Mississippi, called Grand Gulf.

June 17 A young PR man made a reputation by keeping the sheriff from cursing or making obscene gestures and rendering him almost dignified.

HELLO -I'M JUDY PETTY-I'M RUNNING FOR CONGRESS AND I'D APPRECIATE YOUR··· OH, MY-IS THIS THE OLD GUARD REST HOME? WHAT HANDSOME INMATES···UH, I MEAN RESIDENTS!
JUDY! THE PROUD LI'L FLOWER OF TH' G.O.P.! IF THERE'S ANYTHING I CAN DO TO HELP...
FRANK! FOR HER SAKE, DON'T DO HER ANY FAVORS!
GENTLEMEN, THE TIME HAS COME TO CONSIDER THE OUTCOME OF THE ROBINSON-PETTY-TAYLOR RACE-IF ROBINSON LOSES, HE'D BE A CANDIDATE FOR THE REST HOME. OR, IF MS. PETTY LOSES, SHE MIGHT WANT TO MOVE INTO OUR HAVEN OF REST -A DECISION OF PIVOTAL IMPORT, TO SAY THE LEAST!
NOW WAIT JUST A DAD-GUM MINUTE-IF THAT ROBINSON GUY MOVES IN, HE'D BETTER REALIZE THAT AS RESIDENT SHERIFF, I OUTRANK HIM! I'M THE RANKEST LAW MAN AROUND HERE!
THE LESS SAID ABOUT THE SECOND CONGRESSIONAL DISTRICT RACE THE BETTER-BOYCE, GET ME AN ASPIRIN!
NOTHING IN THE RULES ABOUT FEMALE MEMBERSHIP -HMM- I WONDER IF SHE CAN COOK.
COMIN' UP, BROTHER.
OLD GUARD RULE BOOK
ASININE!
THE LOSER GETS TO COME HERE-THAT'S GOT TO HAVE SOME MEANING

June 28

Texas wants our water
WEST TEXAS LAND BARONS' RELIEF FUND
Middle South wants our dough
GIVE TO THE GRAND GOOF RESCUE MISSION
Now we've heard from Three Mile Island
PITCH IN
HELP CLEAN UP OUR MESS
Please say it isn't so!

June 29

July 29 Bethune led a congressional fight to curtail low-interest loans to a "special interest," the electric co-operatives serving rural Arkansas.

Youth Elixir

Hair on a Billiard Ball

Cure for the Common Cold

Lead into Gold

Perpetual Motion

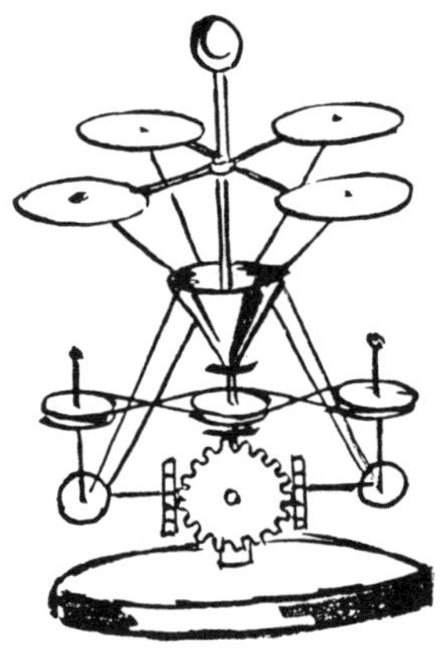

Cheap Nuclear Power

August 3

GENTLEMEN OF THE OLD GUARD REST HOME, I'M DARRELL GLASCOCK AND I BELIEVE YOU'VE MET OUR NEXT CONGRESSMAN, TOMMY ROBINSON. DON'T BE BASHFUL — GIVE THEM ONE OF YOUR LITTLE CARDS, TOMMY.
WELL, HE WON'T BEAT OUR PROUD LITTLE FLOWER OF TH' GOP, JUDY PETTY, IF I'M ANY PROGNOSTICATOR IN POLITICAL EVENTS!
HOLD IT THERE! IF JUDY LOSES, AN' IF JIM JOHNSON LOSES, AN' IF ED BETHUNE LOSES, WE COULD HAVE FOUR REPUBLICANS AT THIS PLACE! IF THAT KEEPS UP, SOME DAY THEY MIGHT BE IN TH' MAJORITY!
IF THAT HAPPENS, WE COULD PUT 'EM IN TH' CAVE DOWN BY TH' RIVER!
GENTLEMEN, LET US NOT WRANGLE OVER THE VICISSITUDES OF PARTY LOYALTY - I MUST CONFESS THAT THE OLDER I GET, THE MORE REPUBLICAN I FEEL.
MY HEART BLEEDS FOR YOU POOR VOTERS - I ONLY GET TICKS, FLEAS AND WORMS.

August 5

August 22 Sheriff Robinson and a former opponent were stopped for speeding at the same place a few days apart, with far different outcomes.

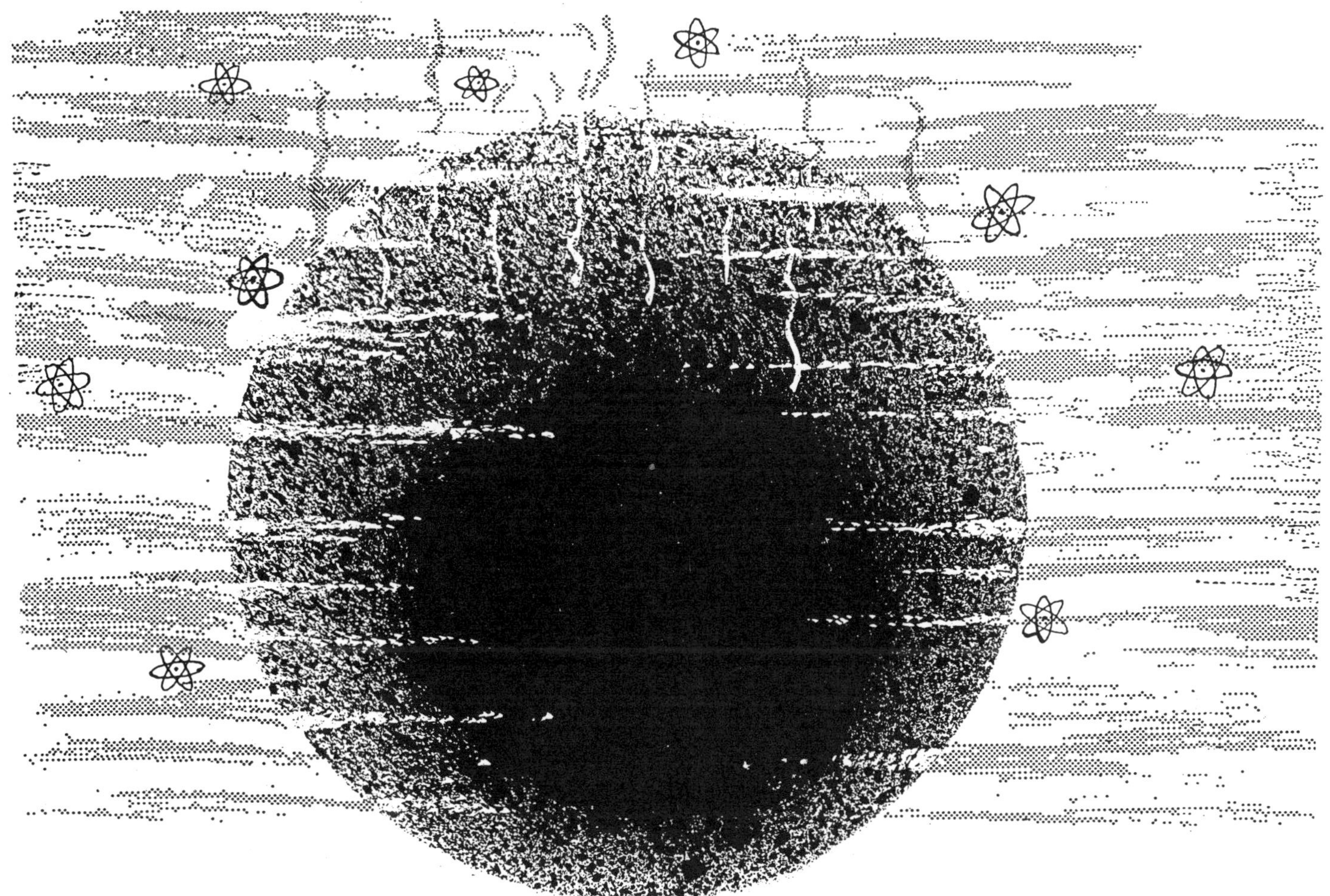

Judy Petty says some things are worse than war.

August 23 Judy Petty addressed the Republican National Convention on national television and made a celebrated remark.

WELL, DIDN'T I PROMISE TO GET THE GOVERNMENT OFF YOUR BACKS?
FERC STAFF
FCC
PHONE RATE HIKE
GRAND GULF AND WATERFORD PAYMENT THREATS
ARK. PSC
ARK. RATE PAYERS

September 5

September 27 Bethune's notions about an independent federal judiciary didn't exactly comport with those of his party's spiritual father.

October 9 Senator Bumpers and Congressman Anthony, who championed different constituencies, worked out a one-sided compromise on the Arkansas wilderness bill.

October 16 Everyone else had been accused, so Bethune charged that Pryor was the one responsible for Arkansas's having to help pay for Grand Gulf.

October 24 The GOP sent a string of national figures to Arkansas to embrace Bethune.

ARE MY OLD EYES PLAYING TRICKS ON ME? THAT COULDN'T BE... YES, IT IS! IT'S **PRESIDENT REAGAN** RIGHT HERE AT THE **OLD GUARD REST HOME!**
GENTLEMEN, I'M HERE TO HELP ELECT AS MANY REPUBLICANS AS POSSIBLE – I'M TOLD THAT THIS PLACE IS THE **HUB OF POLITICAL POWER** IN ARKANSAS.
HAVING AUDIENCE WITH PRESIDENTS IS NOT NOVEL TO ME – I, AS GOVERNOR, ONCE CONFERRED AT LENGTH WITH **IKE** ON HOW WE COULD SOLVE THE INTEGRATION CRISIS IN ARKANSAS!
HUB OF POWER IS RIGHT, BUT I DON'T COTTON TO **COATTAIL CANDIDATES**, 'SPECIALLY REPUBLICANS.
ASININE!
OL' FRANK JUST SWALLERED HIS BANANA-PEEL AN' ALL!
DON'T LOOK AT ME – I WOULDN'T KNOW A PRESIDENT FROM A GRADE "B" ACTOR

November 2

LOOK WHO I FOUND AT THE GATE! SOMEBODY WHEELED HIM IN DURING THE NIGHT!
I CAN'T UNDERSTAND WHAT WENT WRONG! I DID ALL THE RIGHT THINGS- KICKED AROUND FEDERAL JUDGES AND THE AR-KIN-SAS GAZETTE, EXPLOITED THE ABORTION ISSUE, DIDN'T MENTION SEGREGATION, QUOTED THE BIBLE, GOT ENDORSED BY JERRY FALWELL, SHOOK HANDS WITH THE COLOREDS AS WELL AS RONALD REAGAN - I EVEN CHANGED PARTIES!
GENTLEMEN- LET US FORGET WHAT HAPPENED TUESDAY AND THINK ABOUT THE FUTURE - I'M SPEAKING OF THE POSSIBLE APPLICATION OF JUDY PETTY AND ED BETHUNE TO ENTER THE OLD GUARD REST HOME-REMEMBER OUR CREED-"GIVE US YOUR RETIRED, YOUR VANQUISHED, YOUR HUDDLED LOSERS YEARNING TO BREATHE FREE IN SMOKE-FILLED ROOMS, THE WRETCHED REFUSE OF YOUR PLEBISCITES. SEND THESE, THE HOMELESS, TEMPEST-TOSSED TO US; I LIFT MY..." UH... HOW DOES THE REST GO?
YOU SHOULDA CHANGED YOUR NAME TOO, JIM!
YOU MEAN HE'S BEEN DEFEATED BEFORE?
..."LAMP BESIDE THE GOLDEN DOOR"- BUT THAT PART'S CORNY
JIM'S BEEN TURNED DOWN MORE TIMES THAN AN ARMY BLANKET
WILL JUDY AND ED APPLY? IF SO, WILL THEY BE ACCEPTED? DON'T GO 'WAY.

November 8

JUDY PETTY AND ED BETHUNE JUST CALLED IN ON THE STORE PHONE, MEN, AND APPLIED FOR MEMBERSHIP IN THE OLD GUARD REST HOME- WE'RE KINDA CROWDED BUT I GUESS WE'LL HAFTA LET 'EM IN!
NOT NECESSARILY! WE'D HAVE MORE REPUBLICANS AROUND HERE THAN WE GOT CHICKENS! WHY, WE'D HAFTA BUILD SEPARATE QUARTERS FOR 'EM!
AND THAT WOULD TAKE MONEY WHICH WE AIN'T GOT! WE COULD GET ONE OF THEM HOUSING LOANS, BUT YOU KNOW HOW BETHUNE'S AGIN ALL THEM GOV'MENT LOANS!
GENTLEMEN—IN THE INTEREST OF PRAGMATISM, I THINK BROTHER BETHUNE COULD BE PERSUADED TO OVERLOOK HIS IDEOLOGICAL TENETS IN THIS CASE!
A SEPARATE ABODE FOR THE GOP FAITHFUL WHO HAVE FALLEN THROUGH THE SAFETY NET! THE LORD WOULD APPROVE!
CHRISTIAN KINDNESS FOR THE DOWN-AND-OUT REPUBLICANS! I'M ALL CHOKED UP!
SNIFF
SOB
THE POUND'S LOOKING BETTER ALL THE TIME
TO BE DRUG OUT

November 11

I VOTED TO ACCEPT JUDY AND ED BECAUSE ED COULD TEACH US ABOUT TH' TRICKLE DOWN THEORY AND THAT LAUGHIN' CURVE!
THAT'S LAFFER CURVE! BUT I'M READY TO TRY SOME OF JUDY'S COOKIN'— AN' I BET SHE CAN MILK THE COW, TOO!
IF WE'RE GONNA HAVE TO PUT UP WITH THAT BUNCH OF REPUBLICANS, THEY'RE GONNA HAVE TO GET A GOV'MENT LOAN AND BUILD AN ANNEX! WHO DO WE KNOW WITH CLOUT?
GENTLEMEN, I THINK WE NEED TO LOOK NO FURTHER THAN OUR GOOD FRIEND, TOMMY ROBINSON. HE HAS GAINED AN ENVIABLE REPUTATION AS A PARAGON IN ACQUIRING LOANS— INDEED, AMONG THE MEDIA, HE IS SOMETIMES CALLED THE "LOAN ARRANGER."
JUDY PETTY AND ED BETHUNE, I WISH TO ANNOUNCE THAT THE VOTE WAS 6 TO 5 IN FAVOR OF YOUR APPLICATIONS ON CONDITION THAT SEPARATE QUARTERS BE BUILT TO HOUSE YOU FOUR REPUBLICANS. HOW DO YOU FEEL ABOUT GOV'MENT LOANS, ED?
OLD GUARD REST HOME
PURE ASININE!
WELL, AS MY GOOD FRIEND JACK KEMP WOULD SAY...
BLESS YE, ED!
ED'S ON A SABBATICAL— DOIN' A BOOK ON SELECTION OF FEDERAL JUDGES!
HI! I'M JUDY PETTY!
EAT YOUR HEART OUT CONRAD HILTON!

November 14

MR. FAUBUS IS CALLIN' UP TH' **PRESIDENT OF TH' UNITED STATES** ON TH' **STORE PHONE?**
YEP! ORV BELIEVES IN GOIN' STRAIGHT TO TH' **TOP!** HE'S ASKIN' TH' PRESIDENT TO HELP EXPEDITE A GUBMENT LOAN SO JUDY AN' ED AN' THE REST OF US REPUBLICANS CAN BUILD OUR **ANNEX** TO **THE OLD GUARD REST HOME!**
—THAT'S RIGHT, MR. PRESIDENT— JUDY AND ED ASKED ME IF YOU COULD HELP... UH... SIR?... **JUDY PETTY** AND **ED BETHUNE**... REMEMBER?... YOU KNOW... YOU THREW A RALLY FOR THEM IN LITTLE ROCK... HOW'S THAT?... LITTLE ROCK, **ARKANSAS**... ANYWAY...
GIMME THAT PHONE - HE'LL REMEMBER ME—WE SHOOK HANDS ONCE!
I BET THIS IS THE LAST TIME RON WILL ACCEPT A COLLECT CALL FROM THIS PLACE
SOCKS 20¢ PAIR
SEED CORN
WELL BUCKETS
PINTO BEANS
SWEET POTATOES
CRACKERS
LITTLE LIVER PILLS
LYDIA PINKHAM'S COMPOUN
DON'T FORGET TO RING OFF
Chew BROWN MULE
PRINC ALBER

November 18

1985

Under the pressure of extraordinary events, politics undergoes amazing inversions from time to time: for example, **Orval Faubus's** going from the state's leading progressive to the hero of the right in 1957. This was another such year. Congressman **Tommy Robinson**, who had run against arms spending in 1984 ("Reagan never met a weapons system he didn't like"), became one of its loudest champions. **Jim Guy Tucker**, the former attorney general, congressman and utility foe, turned up as Arkansas Power and Light's attorney fighting the Public Service Commission. But those were nothing compared with the transformation of **Bill Clinton**. He sounded and acted like a Republican, promoting tax exemptions and subsidies for business. Though he had been an advocate of investing in roads, he vetoed highway taxes. (But then he pulled his forces back to allow the legislature to override the veto.) Finally, after building a political career baiting AP and L, he became something of an apologist. With Clinton's blessings, the **PSC** suddenly settled a massive rate case by allowing AP and L to phase in higher rates to pay for **Grand Gulf**, something Clinton had vowed to oppose to the finish. **Frank White**, AP and L's old friend and benefactor and a former director in Middle South, became its fiercest critic. AP and L would work for Clinton against White in their election rematch the next year, and its president would become one of his first supporters for president of the United States. Clinton never jumped the utilities again. A strange year, indeed.

February 12 Clinton's advice to the Democratic Party after the 1984 national defeat and his legislative program for industry sounded familiar, and Republican.

EXEMPTIONS
STOCK CERTIFICATES
TAX BREAKS
BONDS
LOOP-HOLES
LEGISLATURE
BECAUSE THEY'RE **BIG**, THAT'S WHY! AND THEY NEED ALL THE HELP THEY CAN GET!

February 22

JUST TO SET THE RECORD STRAIGHT, WHO IS THE INJURED PARTY IN THIS CASE?
LP&L
MP&L
INDUSTRIAL CUSTOMERS
GRAND GULF BANKERS
PSC
MIDDLE SOUTH
AP&L
SMALL RATE PAYERS
GRAND GULF LITIGATION

March 16

March 20 The Arkansas House of Representatives invited Congressman Robinson to speak and then was sorry.

I HAD TO VETO THAT ROAD PROGRAM! THE PEOPLE JUST WEREN'T SOLD ON IT!
WARNING! DANGEROUS ROAD CONDITIONS

March 22

WELL, FRANK, I SEE YOU'RE OFF TO MAKE ANOTHER PASSEL OF SPEECHES ON JUDGE WOODS' RULING TO CONSOLIDATE PULASKI COUNTY SCHOOLS!
YES, I MUST FOLLOW THROUGH ON MY RECENT MEETING WITH THE JUSTICE DEPARTMENT IN WASHINGTON WHERE I I OPENED THE EYES OF WILLIAM BRADFORD REYNOLDS - OR WAS IT REYNOLD BRADFORD WILLIAMS - OR WHOEVER - ABOUT THAT WICKED SCHEME TO CONSOLIDATE TO PREVENT RESEGREGATION OR IS IT DESEGREGATION...? OR WHATEVER!
QUITE FRANKLY, I WORRY ABOUT THE COMPLEXITIES OF TODAY'S PROBLEMS. WHEN THE GREAT CRISIS AROSE IN '57, I JUST CALLED OUT THE NATIONAL GUARD!
YEAH - THESE STICKY PROBLEMS MAKE ME YEARN FOR THE GOOD OL' DAYS!
WELL, MARLIN'S BACK - DIDJA BORROW GOV. BILLY'S TRICYCLE?
YEAH, BUT THESE COUNTRY ROADS ARE MURDER!
Sergeant at Arms ARK. LEGISLATURE
THE GOOD OL' DAYS WERE TOO TRANQUIL FOR SOME PEOPLE

March 28

April 7 The mystery of the times was what happened to Ed Bethune, who disappeared after the election.

May 17 The legislature passed, and Governor Clinton signed, a bill sought by religious fundamentalists to allow people to teach their children in their homes. It is called "home schooling."

May 21 The Reagan administration preached state responsibilities — except when the welfare of utility holding companies was at stake.

IT'S FREELOADERS LIKE YOU THAT ARE CAUSING MOST OF OUR PROBLEMS!
DEFENSE CONTRACTORS
SPECIAL INTEREST TAX SUBSIDIES
CAPITAL GAINS
HIGH INCOME TAX SHELTERS
TR
THE POOR
TAX-FREE MUNICIPAL BONDS
TAX FREE
TAX FREE
HOW DOES HE KEEP GETTING LOOSE?
DARRELL GLASCOCK

May 24

WELL, IF IT AIN'T ED BETHUNE BACK FROM THE CARIBBEAN! WANT ME TO GET YOUR LUGGAGE, ED?
YOU'RE A SIGHT FOR SORE EYES, ED. COULD WE OPEN UP THE FANCY GOP ANNEX OUT BACK?
DON'T HOIST YOUR SAILS WHILE THERE'S NO WIND, MATES. I JUST NEED A PLACE TO DRY-DOCK ME RIG WHILE I SET UP A LAW PRACTICE IN ARGENTA.
WELL, SHIVER ME TIMBERS-AS JACK KEMP WOULD SAY-SQUAWK!
I COULD HELP YOU OUT WITH A FEW REFERRAL CASES, OLD FRIEND.
WHAT DOES ARGENTA NEED WITH A LAWYER-DON'T THEY HAVE A SHERIFF?
ALTHOUGH I HAVE ENCOUNTERED FOIBLES IN THE LAW, IT IS AN HONORED PROFESSION-AND BROTHER BETHUNE IS A DEDICATED BARRISTER. A SENSE OF DUTY PURSUES HIM EVER. IF WE TAKE TO OURSELVES THE SAILS OF MORNING AND DWELL IN THE UTTERMOST PARTS OF THE SEA, EVEN WHEN DARKNESS COVERS US, THE LIGHT OF OUR OBLIGATIONS IS EVER ATTENDANT.
SUPPLY SIDE
I'D RATHER BE SAILING
IN ARGENTA? ASININE!
OLD GUARD REST HOME
I CAN JUST SEE IT NOW-A SUPPLY SIDE LAW PRACTICE WITH A SAFETY NET FOR THE TRULY NEEDY.

May 28

"IT WOULD BE FUN"*
*CLINTON IN THE ATLANTA CONSTITUTION and JOURNAL

May 30

June 2 We began to hear about a religious, paramilitary organization called The Covenant, the Sword and the Arm of the Lord.

June 4 The legislature passed a bill creating an open-ended tax writeoff for gifts to colleges and universities. Clinton vetoed it but, after a scolding by a lobbyist for the universities, retrieved the bill in the night and "unvetoed" it. Finally realizing the profuse hemorrhaging of state taxes that it would cause, he summoned the legislature into special session to change it.

June 14 Clinton got ready to call a special session, but the attorney general had all the ideas about what to do.

WELL DONE! NOW DELIVER HIS WALLET TO GRAND GULF!
FERC
ARKANSAS RATE PAYERS

June 16

June 20 Clinton had to call a special session almost immediately to mitigate somewhat the harm he and the legislature had done at the regular session, principally with tax credits and home schools.

IN RESPONSE TO YOUR ENTHUSIASTIC ENCORE...HERE, FOR THE UMPTEENTH TIME, IS THAT TEASING, TAUNTING, TANTALIZING... NERVINA!
NERVE GAS
CLAP CLAP CLAP CLAP CLAP
WOO! WOO!
STOMP
STOMP
PENTAGON

June 21

WELL, MEN, I DID IT – I TOLD AP&L TO COME TAKE OUT THEIR METER – THAT WE JUST AIN'T GONNA HE'P PAY FOR GRAND GULF!
I ALWAYS THOUGHT THEY WERE PRETTY NICE FOLKS AT AP&L – WHEN I WAS GOV'NOR, THEY HELPED ME SCREEN MY PSC APPLICANTS – AND THEY EVEN LET ME USE THEIR AIRPLANE FREE!
DOGGONE IT, I STILL MISS MY 'LECTRIC RAZOR – OUCH!
'MEMBER WHEN YOU AN' ME RAN FOR GOV'NOR BACK IN '54, ORV? AP&L RAISED ITS RATES DURIN' TH' CAMPAIGN! I THREW IN WITH YOU AND YOU WON – THINK WE COULD DO IT AGAIN?
WHEN JOHN D. ROCKEFELLER (COAL OIL JOHNNY) WAS THE GREAT OIL BARON, HE CHARGED US POOR FOLKS ON GREASY CREEK 10¢ A GALLON FOR HIS PRECIOUS COAL OIL! I, PARENTHETICALLY, DEFEATED HIS GRANDSON FOR GOVERNOR. NOW WHAT A PARADOX! AP&L HAS DRIVEN US FROM NUCLEAR POWER TO COAL OIL – AS THE PHILOSOPHER IS WONT TO SAY, THE MORE THINGS CHANGE, THE MORE THEY STAY THE SAME.
25
ICE
50
75
10
COAL OIL
P&G
AP&L – YOU'VE BEEN DULY WARNED!

June 23

June 25

June 28 AP and L officials tried to get Clinton's PSC chairman removed because he was prejudiced against the utility. They failed but got what they wanted.

July 8 Robinson voted with Reagan and attacked his party's leaders and philosophy, but the majority leader made a visit to help him raise money to pay off his huge campaign debt.

July 21

FIRST, THEY WANTED TO SHUT DOWN ONE LAW SCHOOL- BUT THANKS TO GRAND GULF, IT TURNED OUT WE NEEDED A THIRD ONE!
PETTIFOGGER
SCHOOL of UTILITY LAW
Specializing in Utility Rates
Ephriam P. Pettifogger, Founder
NOPSI
IND. CUSTOMERS
MIDDLE SOUTH
AP&L
MP&L
LP&L
PSC

August 20

August 28 When Robinson voted to fund the MX missile, the PAC spigot opened.

HOLD IT, YOU JACKASSES! ER–I MEAN NOBLE FRIENDS– YOU'RE NOT FINISHED, YET!
TR
BANK DEBTS
ADVERTISING DEBTS

September 3

September 11 Clinton agreed for the PSC to settle the Grand Gulf rate case without a full hearing, but blamed the federal courts, saying he feared they would grant AP and L more money if the PSC continued to oppose Arkansas's paying for the plant and the utility sued.

September 12

September 15

September 18 No one accepted blame for Grand Gulf.

September 30 Athletic Director Frank Broyles at the University of Arkansas disqualified a Razorback linebacker from a football award because it was named after a football star who appeared in TV beer commercials.

YOU WILL KEEP PROTECTING ME FROM THESE PESKY PANHANDLERS, WON'T YOU, UNCLE FERC?
I ♥ REAGAN
FERC
I ♥ FERC
POWER COMPANIES
STATES' UTILITY COMMISSIONS

October 6

October 16 Sam Walton of Bentonville became the nation's richest man. The Stephens brothers weren't in it.

WELL, BOYS- AS YOU ALL KNOW, I'M SITTIN' THIS ONE OUT—I'M NOT RUNNIN' FOR ANYTHING. I QUIT MY JOB AND WHIPPED MYSELF INTO **FIGHTING TRIM**- BUT I GUESS, ACCORDING TO MY **POLLS**, I DIDN'T WEAR WELL WITH TH' VOTERS.
NOW YOU'RE STUCK WITH A TRUCKLOAD OF **POSTERS**- I RECKON WE'LL HAFTA PAPER TH' HOUSE WITH 'EM. IT'LL MAKE IT WARMER IN TH' WINTER.
IF WE DO THAT, WE'LL HAFTA TURN 'EM FACE TO TH' WALL- I DON'T WANT TO WAKE UP EVERY MORNIN' LOOKIN' AT NO **REPUBLICAN**!
IF I COULD TONE DOWN THAT UPPITY AR-KIN-SAW GAZETTE, I JUST MIGHT MAKE ANOTHER RUN AT THE **SOOPREME COURT**!
FORGIVE ME IF I UNWITTINGLY DISPLAY A **GLOWING COUNTENANCE**- IT'S BECAUSE I PERCEIVE A **GROUND SWELL** OF **PUBLIC SENTIMENT**, YEARNING TO RETURN SOME SEMBLANCE OF **MATURITY** TO THE OFFICE OF GOVERNOR- AND I'M AS MATURE AS ANYONE AROUND.
OLD GUARD REST HOME
POSTERS
POSTERS
POSTERS
POSTERS
ASININE!
Vote for FRANK WHITE for
Vote for FRANK WHITE for
Vote for FRANK WHITE for
HOPE SPRINGS ETERNAL IN THE HUMAN BREAST.

November 8

November 12 Arkansas Louisiana Gas Company filed for a rate increase, and consumer groups lined up to testify for it.

November 13 Clinton and the legislature knew that the bewildering property-tax amendment they put over in 1980 had fouled up the tax system but they couldn't decide how it could be corrected.

November 14 In short order, former gas executive Sheffield Nelson and Attorney General Steve Clark, Bill Clinton's chief opponents, said they wouldn't run for governor in 1986.

Flight of the Valkyrie

November 19

November 20 Infighting in the Arkansas Republican Party eventually led to the chairman's resignation.

December 12 Governor Clinton's plan to test all teachers for basic competency was beset by a string of embarrassing blunders.

1986

It was the 150th anniversary of statehood. While people celebrated festively and reflected on the past, their nostalgia was sentimental, not philosophical. Given a chance to invoke the past, they didn't. **Orval Faubus** ran for governor in the Democratic primaries, his third effort since retiring in 1967. The campaign afforded another generation some familiarity with one of the dark chapters in Arkansas history and its most controversial figure this century, but few wanted to go back. Faubus was defeated resoundingly. **Frank White** also offered himself again, this time as an unlikely populist advocating state ownership of the major power company, but the voters turned him down, too, by almost 2 to 1. The campaign redefined gutter politics. White was humiliated by a sequence of incidents early in the campaign, starting with a public tongue-lashing by a woman on the **Public Service Commission** that left him speechless. The Republicans did send out one new personality, a young federal prosecutor with a bucolic name, Asa, who ran against United States Senator **Dale Bumpers**, but if his face was fresh his philosophy was a throwback. Bumpers also won a landslide. United States Representative **Bill Alexander**, the chief deputy Democratic whip, fell from grace when he took an expensive flight on an Air Force plane to Brazil. Republicans tried to knock him off in the Democratic primary and came close, but under their own banner Republicans didn't come close to winning major offices — except one, that held by **John Paul Hammerschmidt**, naturally. It had been pretty much that way for 150 years. Republicans thought people invoked the past too faithfully.

January 12 White had announced in 1985 that he would not run for any office in 1986 but Arkansans' persistent unhappiness over Grand Gulf made him wonder.

January 30 The spaceship Challenger exploded after launch, killing the seven American astronauts.

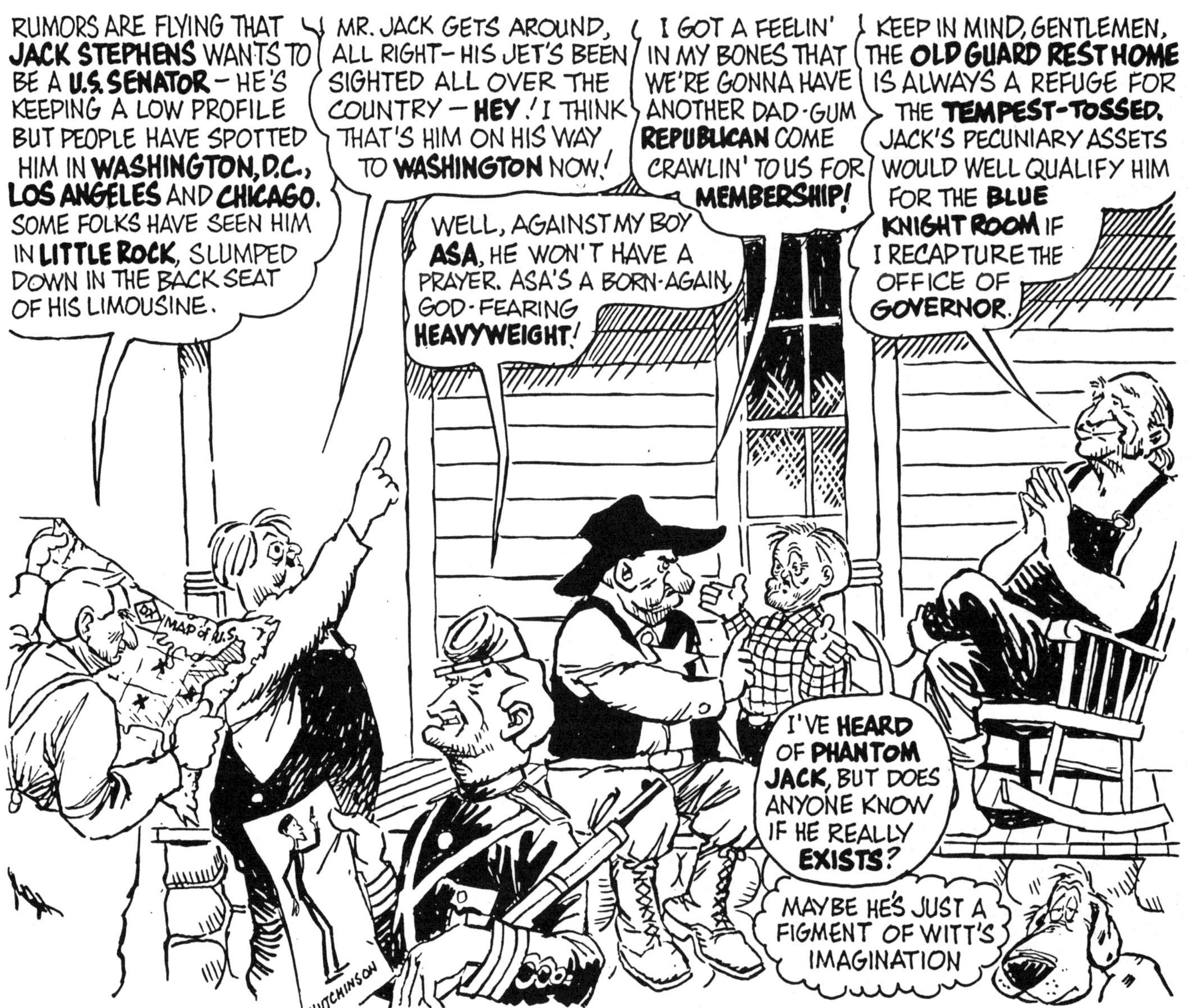

February 4 Jack Stephens of the famous financier brothers, who was something of a recluse, toyed with the notion of running for the United States Senate.

February 5 Though still $275,000 in debt to his advertising agency for his 1984 campaign, Robinson hired the agency for the 1986 race.

IT'S A JUNGLE OUT THERE!
Stephens, Inc.
I WON'T RUN STATEMENT
JACKSON T. STEPHENS
SLAM

February 18

March 2 The National Rifle Association gave Robinson $4,950 for his campaign, and the next day he signed on as a sponsor of its bill to make it easier to buy cheap handguns and harder for lawmen to trace them.

March 30 Orval E. Faubus started his third attempt at a comeback.

OF COURSE, YOUR AVERAGE CONGRESSMAN WOULD BE CORRUPTED BY ALL THIS!
UTILITIES
NEA
TEAMSTERS
MILITARY CONTRS.
UNIONS
GUN LOBBY
SUGAR LOBBY
FLORIDA DEVELOPERS
TOBACCO LOBBY
TR
PAC MONEY
PAC MONEY

April 10

April 11 White had trouble finding an issue on which he wasn't vulnerable himself.

April 22 The Arkansas Education Association endorsed White in the Republican primary.

YOU HAVE THE RIGHT TO REMAIN SILENT...
FELINE PATROL
NEWS ITEM:
NORTH LITTLE ROCK MAYOR PROPOSES CAT LEASH ORDINANCE

May 8

May 14 Caviar of sturgeon harvested from the White River became the rage in New York.

May 16 Darrell Glascock turned up again in his role as political mastermind, this time for Jim Wood, an obscure state senator who challenged United States Representative Bill Alexander in the Democratic primary.

May 18 Faubus said the newspapers didn't tell the truth about him.

May 25 The Republican Congressional Campaign Committee tried to influence the Democratic primary with a last-minute contest to embarrass Alexander. The winner would receive a Republican-paid trip anywhere in the world.

June 1 Bill Clinton won a heavy endorsement in the Democratic primary over Faubus and Dean Goldsby.

IT'S W. DEAN GOLDSBY A LOSER IN THE DEMOCRATIC PRIMARY—SAYS HE WANTS TO APPLY FOR MEMBERSHIP IN THE OLD GUARD REST HOME!
WELL... HE IS A DEMOCRAT AND HE WAS ON THE' SAME TICKET WITH ORV TO HELP UNSEAT THAT KID
BOOM
WHAT ABOUT THIS, ORV—DON'T TH' RULES SAY YOU GOTTA ONCE BE AN ELECTED OFFICIAL?
CHECK MY EYES, BOYCE!
THERE'S NO NEED TO WRANGLE OVER THE VICISSITUDES OF RIGID RULES—I THINK LOGIC SHOULD PREVAIL HERE. ALTHOUGH I HAVE NO PREJUDICE, I REALIZE THE ARRANGEMENT WOULD LEAD TO POSSIBLE UNREST AMONG OUR BROTHERS. IN THE INTEREST OF PEACE AND SAFETY HIS APPLICATION SHOULD BE DENIED.
ASININE!
WELL, THIS TIME HE CAN'T CALL OUT THE GUARD—OH, I FORGOT—THERE'S JIM.

June 4

I'VE UNCOVERED A NUMBER OF PROBLEMS: FIRST, WE'RE NOT VERY BIG—AND SECOND...
PARTY CHAIRMAN LEN BLAYLOCK
ARKANSAS ★GOP★
MODERATES
FAR RIGHT

June 5

June 15

June 18 Glascock found his second loser of the year.

June 20 Reagan boasted of the prosperity he had brought.

July 2 The chairman of the PSC, who once bearded AP and L almost daily, seemed to hibernate after the Grand Gulf settlement.

July 6 White went to a PSC hearing to score some points on Grand Gulf but was fiercely rebuked by Patricia Qualls, a normally meek music teacher who served on the commission. The spectacle finished him as a serious candidate.

July 22 The humiliation continued when Glascock, who had been convicted of drunken driving, arranged for a friend to impersonate him in classes he was supposed to attend as part of his court-ordered punishment.

August 1 Clinton couldn't make up his mind whether to assemble the legislature to deal with a school funding crisis with an election approaching.

August 21 The University of Arkansas sports information director refused to send information to Playboy for its annual college football issue, owing to the magazine's godlessness.

Citizen White
FOR SCHOOL
CONSOLIDATION

Candidate White
AGAINST SCHOOL
CONSOLIDATION

August 26

August 28 Clinton's 40th birthday party, a big campaign event, became an embarrassment when it was learned that literature promoting the party was circulated in government offices.

September 2 Profiles in courage.

Front Runner

September 9 Learning that White planned to take a urine test for drugs and challenge him, Clinton got the jump on him by taking the test first — along with his wife and campaign manager.

September 23 The director of the state Pollution Control and Ecology Department approved a sanitary landfill at Pindall near the Buffalo National River.

September 26 The Federal Election Commission concluded that unsecured bank loans to Robinson's campaign in 1984 were illegal, but it decided to do nothing about it.

September 28

September 30 Little Rock interests liked the idea of North Little Rock building and financing a giant sports and convention arena, but North Little Rock voters didn't.

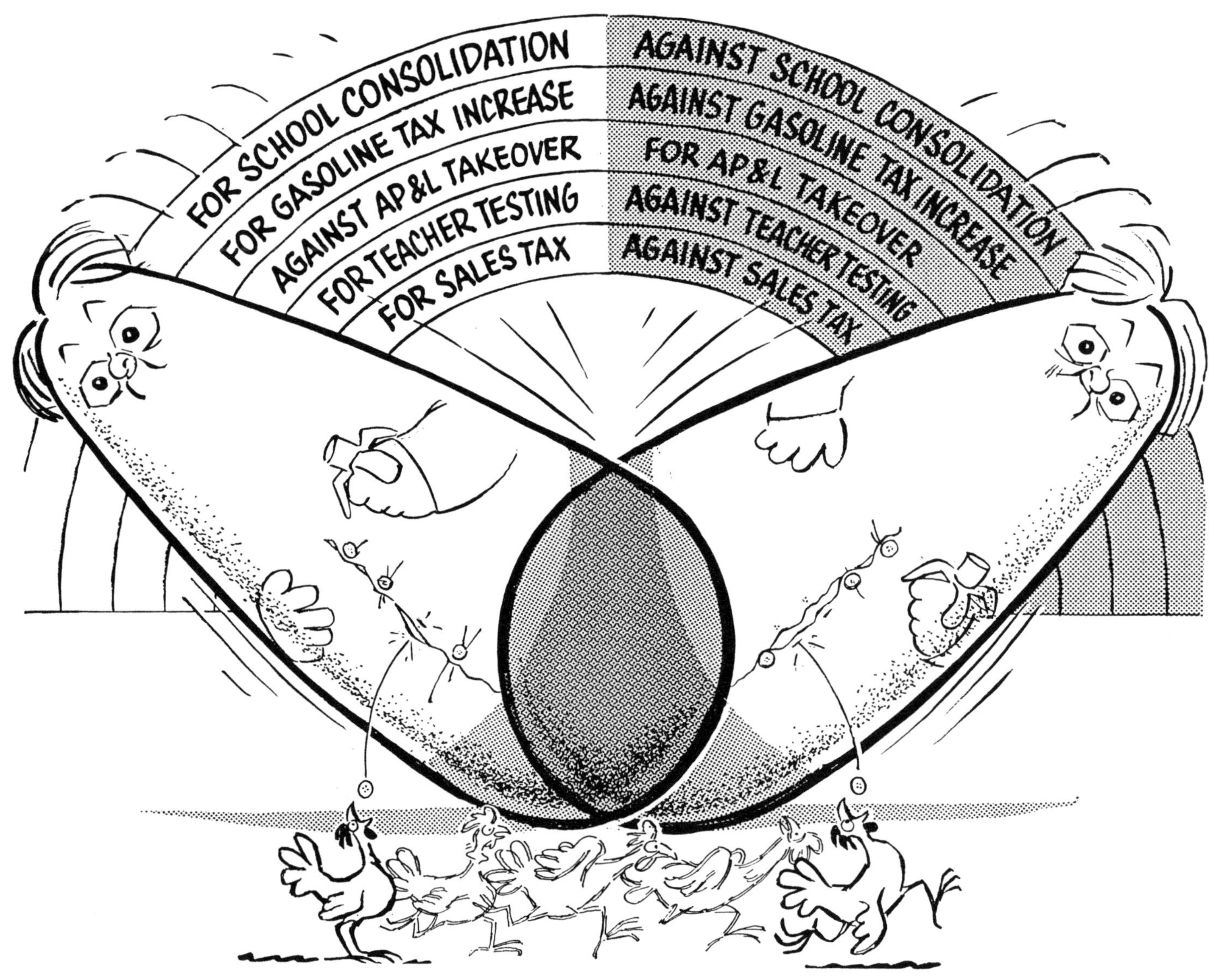

October 3 White had a credibility problem: his past.

IT'S SUPPOSED TO GO THE OTHER WAY! CAN'T YOU DO ANYTHING RIGHT?
CLINTON FOR GOV.

October 9

October 12 The candidates tried to tarnish each other with links to Little Rock financial houses that did heavy business with the state government.

October 16 The gubernatorial campaign was the dirtiest in memory.

October 21 There were renewed proposals for navigation work on the White River.

October 22 The Republican opponent of Senator Dale Bumpers raised a million dollars but not a lot came from Arkansas.

October 31 At the last minute, White tried to link Clinton with the cocaine scandals at the Lasater investment house that sent Lasater and others to prison. Clinton's brother, a former cocaine dealer, had gotten a loan from Lasater. That backfired, too.

AWRIGHT, YOU GUYS! OUTA TH' WAY! I'M DUMPIN' FRANK OFF SO I CAN GET BACK TO MY **PUBLIC RELATIONS** BUSINESS!
I'M OUTA HERE!
YOU HEAR ME, DARRELL? IT'S BACK TO THE FRONT LINES! THERE'S STILL A LOTTA VOTES OUT THERE! WHY, PLACES LIKE **COCKLEBUR** AND **MONKEY RUN** AIN'T BEEN HEARD FROM YET!
POOR FRANK· HOW MUCH MORE CAN HE TAKE? HE WAS JUST GETTIN' HEALED FROM HIS RUN-IN WITH **PAT QUALLS!**
MAYBE WHEN HE COMES AROUND, HE CAN TELL US HOW MY BOY ASA CAME OUT!
YOU GOT A LONG WAIT, JIM- 'CAUSE I THINK HIS **LIGHT BULB** HAS GONE OUT.
I, TOO, SUFFERED TRAUMA FROM MULTIPLE DEFEATS, AND IT IS MY EXPERIENCE THAT **LUCIDITY** EVENTUALLY RETURNS—AND THE PAIN IS REPLACED BY A PHILOSOPHICAL ACCEPTANCE OF LIFE'S HARSH REALITIES.
OLD GUARD REST HOME
IF THIS PLACE IS LUCID, WELCOME TO THE BROOKINGS INSTITUTION

November 6

November 12 The Air Force court-martialed a female officer for having sex and fraternizing with an officer and an enlisted man.

November 21 Faubus took his third wife.

WELL, WE CAN'T FEED EVERYBODY! WILL SOMEONE CLOSE THOSE DRAPES?
HUMAN SERVICES
BUDGET
STATE SERVICES

November 27

December 4 After a disastrous election, Ed Bethune took over the chairmanship of the Republican Party.

IT WAS DOWNRIGHT GOOD OF YOU BOYS TO CLEAN OUT TH' HAY AND CHICKENS FROM THE ABANDONED GOP ANNEX OUT BACK SO THAT ORV AN' HIS NEW BRIDE CAN HAVE A NICE PLACE TO LIVE.
COURSE, WE'D DO THAT FOR ANYBODY – US REPUBLICANS HAVE GOT HEARTS AS BIG AS ALL OUTDOORS
YEAH - ABOUT AS ENORMOUS AS TH' SIZE OF TH' VOTE YA'LL GOT IN NOVEMBER
SOMEHOW I KNEW SHE WAS A GOOD SOUTHERN GIRL – I ALWAYS HAVE BEEN PARTIAL TO GINGHAM CURTAINS
ME AND JAN HAVE COME TO STAY
SO LISTEN WOT I GOT TO SAY
LIFE IS GREAT AND LOVE'S A JOY
THE WORLD YOU SEE IS OUR BIG TOY
ALL JOIN HANDS AND DANCE A JIG
THERE'S NOTHING NOW THAT I CAN'T DIG
DON'T BE GLUM BOYS - LOOK AT ME
A LIVING, JIVING FANTASY!
OLD GUARD REST HOME
SNAP!
SNAP!
LOVE
DON'T LOOK NOW, BUT I THINK I SEE A TRUANT OFFICER

December 7

December 16 The state had to start cutting services. One reason was a tax system badly riddled with advantages for special interests the past decade.

No Arkansan had run for president since, well, since **Wilbur D. Mills** in 1972. Now the state seemed likely to have an embarrassment of riches: *two* candidates for the Democratic nomination. But it was not to be. As he had in 1983, **Senator Bumpers** went to key states, picked up congressional and financial support — and backed out. He was bothered by a lame knee, an old sports injury aggravated by toting firewood and then a surgeon's knife, but he said mainly the whole business would just change his and his family's lives, forever. But that was precisely what appealed to **Bill Clinton**. His problem was different. He was not looking exactly presidential, or even gubernatorial. With the state facing crushing problems — a faltering economy, a diminishing treasury, bankrupt schools and colleges, overflowing prisons, reduced medical services for the poor — the legislature assembled. Clinton was uncertain and, some thought, preoccupied with the national race. Far into the session, when patience was worn thin, he finally started a push for a patchwork of tax bills, but he was no match for the corporate lobbyists who controlled the legislature. The legislature adjourned to await his call for an emergency session to try again. Matters were not made to order for a presidential candidate, who needed to be in Iowa.

January 7 North Little Rock's energetic mayor, Terry Hartwick, suddenly began having troubles: purchasing scandals, a costly romance (for the city treasury and his political stature), run-ins with reporters. This is endemic to the office.

January 8 A panel of appellate judges upheld the Federal Energy Regulatory Commission's order holding AP and L liable for the largest share of Grand Gulf.

News Item: The Arkansas Legislature is due to hit the Capital City early Monday.

January 11

January 20 Representative John E. Miller revived an old plan for a government office complex on the Capitol grounds, a giant addition to the Big Mac Building.

February 10 Clinton's inattention allowed state Senator Nick Wilson, his chief critic, to fill a vacancy in higher education with his own appointee.

February 19 Clinton's education director embarrassed him by granting a superintendent who had failed the governor's controversial teacher test the privilege of taking it again in the privacy of the director's office.

February 26 The legislature passed a bill imposing stiff qualifications for attorney general. It was aimed at stopping a young critic of AP and L who was rumored as a candidate in 1990. Clinton vetoed it.

ME? RUN FOR PRESIDENT? WHY, YES, I HAVE HEARD IT MENTIONED – HARK! I THINK I HEAR IT AGAIN!
STATE'S VITAL NEEDS
GENERAL ASSEMBLY

March 3

GENERAL ASSEMBLY
SNOOKY
THIS IS YOUR CAPTAIN SPEAKING—THE GOOD NEWS IS, WE'RE MAKING EXCELLENT TIME—THE BAD NEWS IS, WE'RE LOST!

March 5

March 13 Bumpers acted like a candidate for president all winter but wouldn't say.

March 31

April 3 While his program hung in the balance, Clinton made a secret trip to California for a weekend with television producer Norman Lear and others who were looking for a presidential candidate. He explained that he was giving legislators a break from his importuning.

April 7 Comparing himself with General Grant at the siege of Vicksburg, Clinton told legislators he would hold them there indefinitely to pass taxes. They quickly defeated his bills and went home.

April 12 Clinton went to Washington, D.C., leaving his nemesis Wilson as acting governor. Wilson demoted the chief of staff, made many appointments and scorned the governor.

April 14 The legislature passed, and Governor Clinton signed, a bill shielding motor fuel tax records from the public. Among the records shielded were those of the legislation's mover, a major fuel distributor.

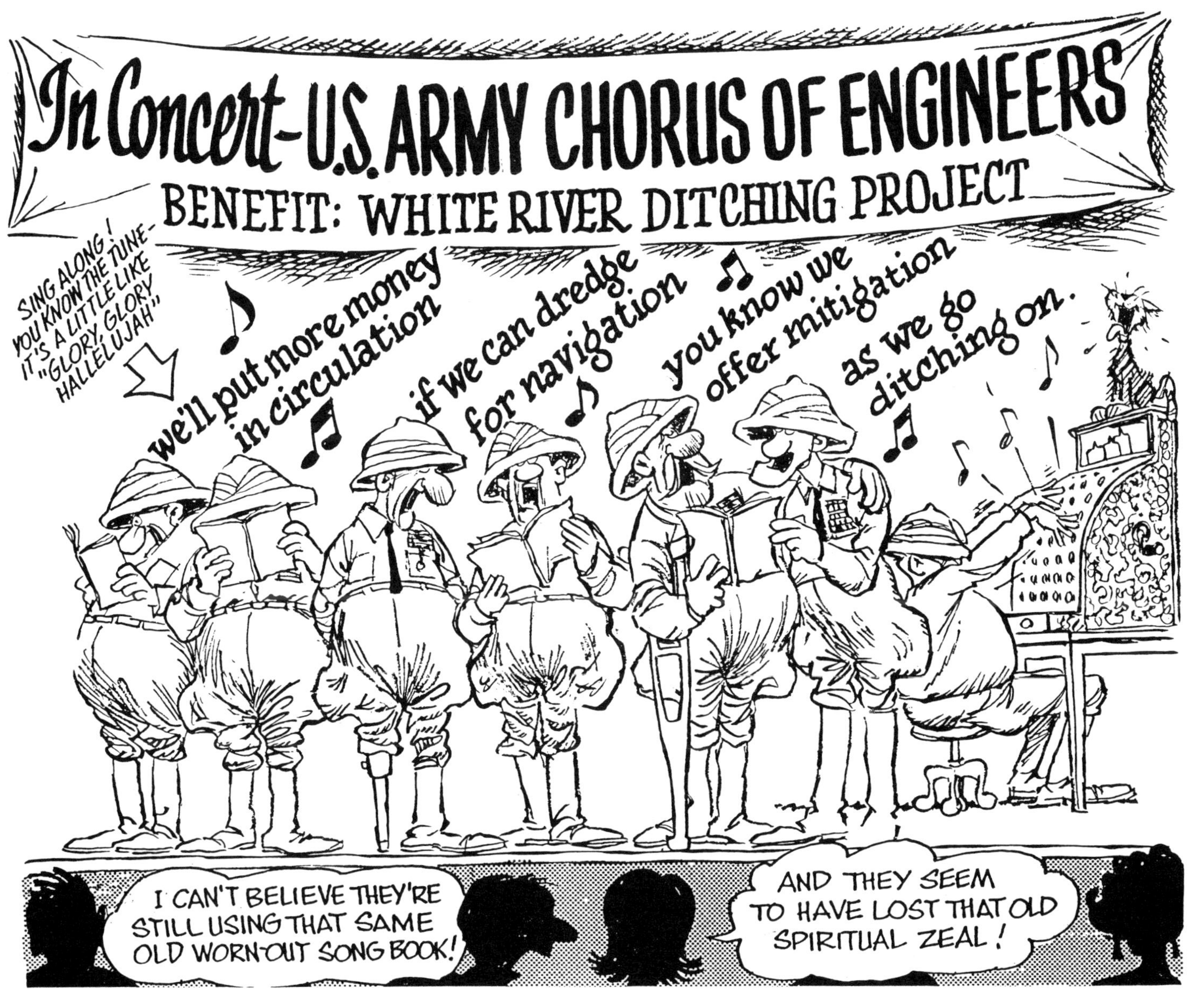
In Concert-U.S. ARMY CHORUS OF ENGINEERS
BENEFIT: WHITE RIVER DITCHING PROJECT
SING ALONG! YOU KNOW THE TUNE-IT'S A LITTLE LIKE "GLORY, GLORY HALLELUJAH"
we'll put more money in circulation
if we can dredge for navigation
you know we offer mitigation
as we go ditching on.
I CAN'T BELIEVE THEY'RE STILL USING THAT SAME OLD WORN-OUT SONG BOOK!
AND THEY SEEM TO HAVE LOST THAT OLD SPIRITUAL ZEAL!

April 15

HEY – IT DOESN'T HAVE A **MOTOR**!
OR A **DRIVER**!
FORWARD ARKANSAS
Arkansas is a Natural
LAND OF OPPORTUNITY

April 16

April 19 (Easter)

UNFINISHED BUSINESS
THERE SHE GOES – YOU CAN COME ON OUT NOW, IT ONLY HITS EVERY COUPLE OF YEARS!
76th GENERAL ASSEMBLY
LAW MAKERS

April 21

May 5 The Arkansas State Chamber of Commerce called the legislative session a big success.

May 8 The Army announced it wanted to use the Ouachita and Ozark National Forests for light infantry training. Congressman Tommy Robinson, a member of the Armed Services Committee, supported the plan, but environmentalists fiercely opposed it.

May 17 North Little Rock Mayor Terry Hartwick became the subject of a prosecutor's investigation after taking numerous trips to exotic places paid for by contractors doing business with the city and in the company of a college majorette. He called them business trips.

George Fisher

George Fisher's cartoons have caused comment since the day his father found the first one painted on the side of their house in Beebe, Arkansas. Then, his drawing was a personal matter. Now he comments on the local and national scenes as chief editorial cartoonist for the Arkansas Gazette.

Though art has always been Fisher's medium, it was the school desegregation crises of the Faubus years that prompted him to leave his commercial studio and portray the political scene. Since then, there has been no reason to stop, and Fisher's view of the world continues to draw a reaction from loyal followers. Many also take the time to search for the hidden name "Snooky," as George called his late wife, whom he met in England during World War II.

Fisher, who lives in Little Rock, has received numerous honors for his editorial cartoons, including first and second place awards from the National Newspaper Association and others from the American Civil Liberties Union, The National Conference of Christians and Jews, and the National Wildlife Federation. A more personal distinction comes from the Rackensack Folklore Society of Central Arkansas, an organization of musicians co-founded by Fisher which celebrates its 25th anniversary in 1988.

Photo: Kay Danielson